365
ONE-MINUTE MEDITATIONS

My Utmost for His Highest

FROM THE POWERFUL, UPDATED
DEVOTIONAL BY OSWALD CHAMBERS

365
ONE-MINUTE MEDITATIONS

MY UTMOST FOR HIS HIGHEST

FROM THE POWERFUL, UPDATED DEVOTIONAL BY OSWALD CHAMBERS

BARBOUR
PUBLISHING

These selections from *My Utmost for His Highest* by Oswald Chambers, edited by James Reimann, are published by special arrangement with and permission of Discovery House Publishers, Grand Rapids, Michigan 49501. ©1992 by Oswald Chambers Publications Assn., Ltd. Original edition ©1935 by Dodd, Mead & Co., Inc. ©1963 renewed by Oswald Chambers Publications Assn., Ltd. All rights reserved.

Editorial assistance by Jennifer Hahn.

ISBN 978-1-60260-388-2

Published by Barbour Publishing, Inc., P.O. Box 719, Uhrichsville, Ohio 44683, www.barbourbooks.com

Our mission is to publish and distribute inspirational products offering exceptional value and biblical encouragement to the masses.

Member of the
Evangelical Christian
Publishers Association

Printed in the United States of America.

A MINUTE A DAY CAN CHANGE YOUR LIFE.

We're all busy and pressed for time. But somewhere in our daily schedule, there must be at least sixty free seconds.

Look for that open minute and fill it with this book. *365 One-Minute Meditations: My Utmost for His Highest* provides a quick but powerful reading for every day of the year, promising real spiritual impact. Each day's entry features a carefully selected verse from God's Word, along with a condensed reading from *My Utmost*, one of the most beloved devotionals of all time.

First published some seventy-five years ago, *My Utmost for His Highest* is still changing lives with its challenging message of commitment to God. These excerpts are taken from the updated edition of the book edited by James Reimann.

If you're seeking a spiritual lift, try *365 One-Minute Meditations: My Utmost for His Highest*. You'll only need a moment per day—but the benefits could be life-changing.

LET US KEEP TO THE POINT

My earnest expectation and hope
that in nothing I shall be ashamed,
but with all boldness, as always,
so now also Christ will be magnified
in my body, whether by life or by death.

PHILIPPIANS 1:20

When we think seriously about what it will cost others if we obey the call of Jesus, we tell God He doesn't know what our obedience will mean. Keep to the point—He does know. Shut out every other thought and keep yourself before God in this one thing only—my utmost for His highest. I am determined to be absolutely and entirely for Him and Him alone.

WILL YOU GO OUT WITHOUT KNOWING?

He went out, not knowing where he was going.
HEBREWS 11:8

Have you ever "gone out" in this way? If so, there is no logical answer possible when anyone asks you what you are doing. One of the most difficult questions to answer in Christian work is "What do you expect to do?" You don't know what you are going to do. The only thing you know is that God knows what He is doing.

"CLOUDS AND DARKNESS"

Clouds and darkness surround Him.

PSALM 97:2

A person who has not been born again by the Spirit of God will tell you that the teachings of Jesus are simple. But when he is baptized by the Holy Spirit, he finds that "clouds and darkness surround Him." When we come into close contact with the teachings of Jesus Christ, we have our first realization of this. The only possible way to have full understanding of the teachings of Jesus is through the light of the Spirit of God shining inside us.

"WHY CAN I NOT FOLLOW YOU NOW?"

Peter said to Him, "Lord, why can I not follow You now?"
JOHN 13:37

There are times when you can't understand why you cannot do what you want to do. When God brings a time of waiting and appears to be unresponsive, don't fill it with busyness; just wait. The time of waiting may come to teach you the meaning of sanctification—to be set apart from sin and made holy—or it may come after the process of sanctification has begun to teach you what service means. Never run before God gives you His direction.

THE LIFE OF POWER TO FOLLOW

Jesus answered him,
"Where I am going you cannot follow Me now,
but you shall follow Me afterward."

JOHN 13:36

Three years earlier Jesus had said, "Follow Me" (Matthew 4:19), and Peter followed with no hesitation. Later he came to the place where he denied Jesus, and his heart broke. Then he received the Holy Spirit and Jesus said again, "Follow Me" (John 21:19). All our promises and resolutions end in denial because we have no power to accomplish them. When we come to the end of ourselves, not just mentally but completely, we are able to "receive the Holy Spirit."

WORSHIP

He pitched his tent with Bethel
on the west and Ai on the east;
there he built an altar to the LORD.

GENESIS 12:8

Worship is giving God the best that He has given you. Take time to meditate before God and offer the blessing back to Him in a deliberate act of worship. God will never allow you to keep a spiritual blessing completely for yourself. It must be given back to Him so that He can make it a blessing to others.

There are not three levels of spiritual life—worship, waiting, and work. God's idea is that the three should go together as one. They were always together in the life of our Lord and in perfect harmony.

INTIMATE WITH JESUS

*"Have I been with you so long,
and yet you have not known Me?"*

JOHN 14:9

True friendship is rare on earth. It means identifying with someone in thought, heart, and spirit. The whole experience of life is designed to enable us to enter into this closest relationship with Jesus Christ.

The Christian who is truly intimate with Jesus will never draw attention to himself but will only show the evidence of a life where Jesus is completely in control. The picture resulting from such a life is that of the strong, calm balance that our Lord gives to those who are intimate with Him.

IS MY SACRIFICE LIVING?

And Abraham built an altar. . .and he bound Isaac his son.

GENESIS 22:9

God never tells us to give up things just for the sake of giving them up, but He tells us to give them up for the sake of the only thing worth having, namely, life with Himself. It is a matter of loosening the bands that hold back our lives. Those bands are loosened immediately by identification with the death of Jesus.

It is of no value to God to give Him your life for death. He wants you to be a "*living* sacrifice."

PRAYERFUL INNER SEARCHING

May your whole spirit, soul,
and body be preserved blameless.

I THESSALONIANS 5:23

D o we believe that God can fortify and protect our thought processes far beyond where we can go? The cleansing from sin we experience will reach to the heights and depths of our spirit if we will "walk in the light as He is in the light" (1 John 1:7). It is only when we are protected by God with the miraculous sacredness of the Holy Spirit that our spirit, soul, and body can be preserved in pure uprightness until the coming of Jesus.

THE OPENED SIGHT

To open their eyes. . .that they may receive. . .

ACTS 26:18

The only sign that a person is saved is that he has received something from Jesus Christ. When a person is born again, he knows that it is because he has received something as a gift from Almighty God and not because of his own decision. Salvation means that we are brought to the place where we are able to receive something from God on the authority of Jesus Christ, namely, forgiveness of sins.

WHAT MY OBEDIENCE TO GOD COSTS OTHER PEOPLE

They laid hold of a certain man, Simon. . .
and on him they laid the cross.

LUKE 23:26

Because we are so involved in the universal purposes of God, others are immediately affected by our obedience to Him. We can disobey God if we choose, and it will bring immediate relief to the situation, but it will grieve our Lord. If, however, we obey God, He will care for those who have suffered the consequences of our obedience.

HAVE YOU EVER BEEN ALONE WITH GOD?

When they were alone,
He explained all things to His disciples.

MARK 4:34

*O*ur Solitude with Him. We can only be used by God after we allow Him to show us the deep, hidden areas of our own character. Jesus will reveal to us everything we have held within ourselves before His grace began to work.

The only One who understands us is God. Whenever there is any element of pride or conceit remaining, Jesus can't teach us anything. Many things are shown to us, often without effect. But when God gets us alone over them, they will be clear.

HAVE YOU EVER BEEN ALONE WITH GOD?

When He was alone. . .the twelve asked Him.

MARK 4:10

H is Solitude with Us. When God gets us absolutely alone, and we are totally speechless, unable to ask even one question, then He begins to teach us.

As you journey with God, the only thing He intends to be clear is the way He deals with your soul. Are we alone with Him now? Jesus cannot teach us anything until we quiet all our intellectual questions and get alone with Him.

CALLED BY GOD

"Whom shall I send, and who will go for Us?"
Then I said, "Here am I! Send me."

ISAIAH 6:8

M any are called, but few are chosen"
(Matthew 22:14). The chosen ones are
those who have come into a relationship with God
through Jesus Christ and have had their spiritual
condition changed and their ears opened. When
our Lord called His disciples, He did it without
irresistible pressure from the outside. The quiet
yet passionate insistence of His "Follow Me" was
spoken to men whose every sense was receptive.

DO YOU WALK IN WHITE?

*Buried with Him. . .that. . .even so
we also should walk in newness of life.*

ROMANS 6:4

No one experiences complete sanctification
without going through a "white funeral"—
the burial of the old life. Have you really come to
your last days? You have often come to them in
your mind, but have you *really* experienced them?
You cannot die or go to your funeral in a mood of
excitement. Death means you stop being. You must
agree with God and stop being the intensely striving
kind of Christian you have been. It is dying—being
"baptized into His death" (Romans 6:3).

THE VOICE OF THE NATURE OF GOD

I heard the voice of the Lord, saying:
"Whom shall I send?"

ISAIAH 6:8

The call of God is not a reflection of my nature; my personal desires and temperament are of no consideration. As long as I dwell on my own qualities and traits and think about what I am suited for, I will never hear the call of God.

The majority of us cannot hear anything but ourselves. And we cannot hear anything God says. But to be brought to the place where we can hear the call of God is to be profoundly changed.

THE CALL OF THE NATURAL LIFE

But when it pleased God. . .to reveal His Son in me. . .

GALATIANS 1:15-16

The call of God is not a call to serve Him in any particular way. My contact with the nature of God will shape my understanding of His call and will help me realize what I truly desire to do for Him. The call of God is an expression of His nature; the service which results in my life is suited to me and is an expression of my nature.

"It Is the Lord!"

Thomas answered and said to Him,
"My Lord and my God!"

JOHN 20:28

How many of us are expecting Jesus Christ to quench our thirst when we should be satisfying Him! We should be pouring out our lives, investing our total beings, not drawing on Him to satisfy us. That means lives of pure, uncompromising, and unrestrained devotion to the Lord Jesus, which will be satisfying to Him wherever He may send us.

VISION AND DARKNESS

Horror and great darkness fell upon him.

GENESIS 15:12

Whenever God gives a vision to a Christian, it is as if He puts him in "the shadow of His hand" (Isaiah 49:2). The saint's duty is to be still and listen. There is a "darkness" that comes from too much light—that is the time to listen. When God gives you a vision and darkness follows, wait. God will bring the vision He has given you to reality in your life if you will wait on His timing.

ARE YOU FRESH FOR EVERYTHING?

*"Unless one is born again,
he cannot see the kingdom of God."*

JOHN 3:3

Being born again provides a freshness all the time in thinking, talking, and living—a continual surprise of the life of God. Do we feel fresh this very moment, or are we stale, frantically searching our minds for something to do? Freshness is not the result of obedience; it comes from the Holy Spirit.

Being born of the Spirit means much more than we usually think. It gives us new vision and keeps us absolutely fresh for everything through the never-ending supply of the life of God.

RECALL WHAT GOD REMEMBERS

"I remember. . .the kindness of your youth."

JEREMIAH 2:2

Am I as spontaneously kind to God as I used to be, or am I only expecting God to be kind to me? Does everything in my life fill His heart with gladness, or do I constantly complain because things don't seem to be going my way? A person who has forgotten what God treasures will not be filled with joy. How much kindness have I shown Him in the past week?

AM I LOOKING TO GOD?

"Look to Me, and be saved."

ISAIAH 45:22

Do we expect God to come to us with His blessings and save us? The greatest difficulty spiritually is to concentrate on God, and His blessings are what make it so difficult. Troubles almost always make us look to God, but His blessings tend to divert our attention elsewhere.

We will find what we are looking for if we will concentrate on Him. Our difficulties, our trials, and our worries about tomorrow all vanish when we look to God.

TRANSFORMED BY BEHOLDING

*We all, with unveiled face,
beholding as in a mirror the glory of the Lord,
are being transformed into the same image.*

2 CORINTHIANS 3:18

The most important rule for us is to concentrate on keeping our lives open to God. Let everything else be set aside. The busyness of things obscures our concentration on God. We must maintain a position of beholding Him, keeping our lives completely spiritual through and through. Let other things come and go as they will; let other people criticize us as they will; but never allow anything to obscure the life that "is hidden with Christ in God" (Colossians 3:3).

GOD'S OVERPOWERING PURPOSE

"I have appeared to you for this purpose."

ACTS 26:16

I t is important that I learn not to be "disobedient to the heavenly vision"—not to doubt that it can be attained (Acts 26:19). It is not enough to give mental assent to the fact that God has redeemed the world, nor even to know that the Holy Spirit can make all that Jesus did a reality in my life. I must have the foundation of a personal relationship with Him. There would be nothing there without a personal relationship.

LEAVE ROOM FOR GOD

But when it pleased God. . .

GALATIANS 1:15

As servants of God, we must learn to make room for Him. We plan and figure and predict that this or that will happen, but we forget to make room for God to come in as He chooses. The way to make room for Him is to expect Him to come, but not in a certain way. No matter how well we may know God, the great lesson to learn is that He may break in at any minute.

LOOK AGAIN AND CONSECRATE

"If God so clothes the grass of the field...
will He not much more clothe you?"

MATTHEW 6:30

How can we maintain the simplicity of Jesus so that we may understand Him? By receiving His Spirit, recognizing and relying on Him, and obeying Him as He brings us the truth of His Word, life will become amazingly simple.

Consecration is the act of continually separating myself from everything except that which God has appointed me to do. It is not a onetime experience but an ongoing process. Am I continually separating myself and looking to God every day of my life?

LOOK AGAIN AND THINK

"Do not worry about your life."

MATTHEW 6:25

Our Lord says to be careful only about one thing—our relationship to Him. But our common sense says, "That is absurd. I *must* consider how I am going to live, and I *must* consider what I am going to eat and drink." Jesus says you must not. Beware of allowing yourself to think that He says this while not understanding your circumstances. Jesus Christ knows our circumstances better than we do, and He says we must not think about these things to the point where they become the primary concern of our life.

HOW COULD SOMEONE SO PERSECUTE JESUS!

"Saul, Saul, why are you persecuting Me?"

ACTS 26:14

Whenever we are obstinate and self-willed and set on our own ambitions, we are hurting Jesus. Every time we stand on our own rights, we are persecuting Him. Whenever we rely on self-respect, we grieve His Spirit.

All I do should be based on a perfect oneness with Him. This will mean that others may use me, go around me, or completely ignore me, but if I will submit to it for His sake, I will prevent Jesus Christ from being persecuted.

HOW COULD SOMEONE BE SO IGNORANT!

"Who are You, Lord?"

ACTS 26:15

God has to destroy our determined confidence in our own convictions. We say, "I know that this is what I should do"—and suddenly the voice of God speaks in a way that overwhelms us by revealing the depths of our ignorance. We show our ignorance of Him in the very way we decide to serve Him. We serve Jesus in a spirit that is not His and hurt Him by our defense of Him. The spirit of our Lord in His followers is described in 1 Corinthians 13.

THE DILEMMA OF OBEDIENCE

And Samuel was afraid to tell Eli the vision.

I SAMUEL 3:15

God never speaks to us in dramatic ways, but in ways that are easy to misunderstand. Then we say, "I wonder if that is God's voice." Without the sovereign hand of God Himself, nothing touches our lives. Do we discern His hand at work, or do we see things as mere occurrences?

Never ask another person's advice about anything God makes you decide before Him. If you ask advice, you will almost always side with Satan.

DO YOU SEE YOUR CALLING?

Separated to the gospel. . .

ROMANS 1:1

Our calling is not primarily to be holy men and women, but to be proclaimers of the gospel of God. The one all-important thing is that the gospel of God should be recognized as *the* abiding reality. Reality is not human goodness or holiness or heaven or hell—it is redemption. Personal holiness is an effect of redemption, not the cause of it. If we place our faith in human goodness, we will go under when testing comes.

The Call of God

For Christ did not send me to baptize,
but to preach the gospel.

1 Corinthians 1:17

Paul states here that the call of God is to preach the gospel. But remember what Paul means by "the gospel," namely, the reality of redemption in our Lord Jesus Christ. We are inclined to make sanctification the goal of our preaching. Paul refers to personal experiences only by way of illustration, never as the end of the matter. We are not commissioned to preach salvation or sanctification—we are commissioned to lift up Jesus Christ.

THE COMPELLING FORCE OF THE CALL

Woe is me if I do not preach the gospel!

1 CORINTHIANS 9:16

To be "separated to the gospel" means being able to hear the call of God (Romans 1:1). Once someone begins to hear that call, a suffering worthy of the name of Christ is produced. Suddenly, every ambition, every desire of life, and every outlook is completely blotted out and extinguished. Only one thing remains—"*separated to the gospel.*" Woe be to the soul who tries to head in any other direction once that call has come to him.

BECOMING THE "FILTH OF THE WORLD"

We have been made as the filth of the world.

1 CORINTHIANS 4:13

You can refuse to let God count you as one who is "separated to the gospel." Or you can say, "I don't care if I am treated like 'the filth of the world' as long as the gospel is proclaimed." A true servant of Jesus Christ is one who is willing to experience martyrdom for the reality of the gospel of God.

THE COMPELLING MAJESTY OF HIS POWER

For the love of Christ compels us.

2 CORINTHIANS 5:14

When we are born again by the Spirit of God, our testimony is based solely on what God has done for us. But that will change once you "receive power when the Holy Spirit has come upon you" (Acts 1:8). We will accept everything that happens as if it were happening to Him, whether we receive praise or blame, persecution or reward. No one is able to take this stand for Jesus Christ who is not totally compelled by the majesty of His power.

ARE YOU READY TO BE POURED OUT AS AN OFFERING?

*Yes, and if I am being poured out as a drink offering
on the sacrifice and service of your faith,
I am glad and rejoice with you all.*

PHILIPPIANS 2:17

It is one thing to follow God's way of service if you are regarded as a hero, but quite another thing if the road marked out for you by God requires becoming a "doormat" under other people's feet. Are you ready to be sacrificed like that? Are you willing to give and be poured out until you are used up and exhausted—not seeking to be ministered to, but to minister?

ARE YOU READY TO BE POURED OUT AS AN OFFERING?

I am already being poured out as a drink offering.

2 TIMOTHY 4:6

Are you ready to be poured out as an offering? It is an act of your will, not your emotions. *Tell* God you are ready to be offered as a sacrifice for Him. Then accept the consequences as they come, without any complaints, in spite of what God may send your way.

Tell God you are ready to be poured out as an offering, and God will prove Himself to be all you ever dreamed He would be.

SPIRITUAL DEJECTION

But we were hoping. . . . Indeed,
besides all this, today is the third day.

LUKE 24:21

We look for visions from heaven and for earthshaking events to see God's power. Even the fact that we are dejected is proof that we do this. Yet we never realize that all the time God is at work in our everyday events and in the people around us. If we will only obey and do the task that He has placed closest to us, we will see Him. One of the most amazing revelations of God comes to us when we learn that. It is in the everyday things of life that we realize the magnificent deity of Jesus Christ.

THE COST OF SANCTIFICATION

May the God of peace Himself sanctify you completely.

1 THESSALONIANS 5:23

When we pray, asking God to sanctify us, are we prepared to measure up to what that really means? The cost will be a deep restriction of all our earthly concerns, and an extensive cultivation of all our godly concerns. Sanctification means to be intensely focused on God's point of view. It means to secure and to keep all the strength of our body, soul, and spirit for God's purpose alone. Are we really prepared for God to perform in us everything for which He separated us?

ARE YOU EXHAUSTED SPIRITUALLY?

The everlasting God. . .neither faints nor is weary.
ISAIAH 40:28

Have you delivered yourself over to exhaustion because of the way you have been serving God? If so, then renew and rekindle your desires and affections. Examine your reasons for service. Continually look back to the foundation of your love and affection and remember where your Source of power lies. Be exhausted for God, but remember that He is your supply.

IS YOUR ABILITY
TO SEE GOD BLINDED?

*Lift up your eyes on high,
and see who has created these things.*

ISAIAH 40:26

The real test of spiritual focus is being able to bring your mind and thoughts under control. Is your mind focused on the face of an idol? Is the idol yourself? Is it your work? If so, then your ability to see God is blinded. You will be powerless when faced with difficulties and will be forced to endure in darkness. If your power to see has been blinded, don't look back on your own experiences, but look to God. It is God you need.

IS YOUR MIND STAYED ON GOD?

"You will keep him in perfect peace,
whose mind is stayed on You."

ISAIAH 26:3

Your mind is the greatest gift God has given you, and it ought to be devoted entirely to Him. This will be one of the greatest assets of your faith when a time of trial comes, because then your faith and the Spirit of God will work together. You will begin to see that your thoughts are from God as well, and your mind will no longer be at the mercy of your impulsive thinking but will always be used in service to God.

ARE YOU LISTENING TO GOD?

*Then they said to Moses, "You speak with us,
and we will hear; but let not God speak with us, lest we die."*

EXODUS 20:19

We don't consciously and deliberately disobey God—we simply don't listen to Him. God has given His commands to us, but we pay no attention to them—not because of willful disobedience, but because we do not truly love and respect Him.

Am I constantly humiliating God by ignoring Him, while He lovingly continues to treat me as His child? Our real delight in finally hearing Him is tempered with the shame we feel for having taken so long to do so.

THE DEVOTION OF HEARING

"Speak, for Your servant hears."

1 SAMUEL 3:10

The goal of my spiritual life is such close identification with Jesus Christ that I will always hear God and know that God always hears me. If I am united with Jesus Christ, I hear God all the time through the devotion of hearing. What hinders me from hearing is my attention to other things. The attitude of a child of God should always be "Speak, for Your servant hears." Have you heard God's voice today?

THE DISCIPLINE OF HEARING

*"Whatever I tell you in the dark, speak in the light;
and what you hear in the ear, preach on the housetops."*

MATTHEW 10:27

Sometimes God puts us through the experience and discipline of darkness to teach us to hear and obey Him. Pay attention when God puts you into darkness, and keep your mouth closed while you are there. Are you in the dark right now in your circumstances or in your life with God? If so, then remain quiet. Darkness is the time to listen. Don't talk to other people about it; don't read books to find out the reason for the darkness; just listen and obey.

"AM I MY BROTHER'S KEEPER?"

None of us lives to himself.

ROMANS 14:7

Has it ever dawned on you that you are responsible spiritually to God for other people? For instance, if I allow any turning away from God in my private life, everyone around me suffers. If you allow physical selfishness, mental carelessness, moral insensitivity, or spiritual weakness, everyone in contact with you will suffer. But you ask, "Who is sufficient to be able to live up to such a lofty standard?" "Our sufficiency is from God" and God alone (2 Corinthians 3:5).

THE INSPIRATION OF SPIRITUAL INITIATIVE

"Arise from the dead."

EPHESIANS 5:14

When God sends His inspiration, it comes to us with such miraculous power that we are able to "arise from the dead" and do the impossible. The remarkable thing about spiritual initiative is that the life and power come after we "get up and get going." God does not give us overcoming life—He gives us life *as we overcome.* If we will take the initiative to overcome, we will find that we have the inspiration of God, because He immediately gives us the power of life.

TAKING THE INITIATIVE
AGAINST DEPRESSION

"Arise and eat."

1 KINGS 19:5

Depression tends to turn us away from the everyday things of God's creation. But whenever God steps in, His inspiration is to do the most natural, simple things—things we would never have imagined God was in. The inspiration that comes to us in this way is an initiative against depression. But we must take the first step and do it in the inspiration of God. When the Spirit of God leads us instinctively to do something, the moment we do it the depression is gone.

TAKING THE INITIATIVE
AGAINST DESPAIR

"Rise, let us be going."

MATTHEW 26:46

We will have times of despair caused by real events in our lives, and we will be unable to lift ourselves out of them. If we are inspired by God, what is the next thing? It is to trust Him absolutely and to pray on the basis of His redemption. Never let the sense of past failure defeat your next step.

TAKING THE INITIATIVE AGAINST DRUDGERY

Arise, shine.

ISAIAH 60:1

Drudgery is work that is far removed from anything we think of as ideal work. It is the utterly hard, menial, tiresome, and dirty work. The inspiration of God is required if drudgery is to shine with the light of God upon it. In some cases the way a person does a task makes that work sanctified and holy forever. It may be a very common everyday task, but after we have seen it done, it becomes different. When the Lord does something through us, He always transforms it.

TAKING THE INITIATIVE AGAINST DAYDREAMING

"Arise, let us go from here."

JOHN 14:31

Daydreaming about something in order to do it properly is right, but daydreaming about it when we should be doing it is wrong. When our purpose is to seek God and to discover His will for us, daydreaming is right and acceptable. But when our inclination is to spend time daydreaming over what we have already been told to do, it is unacceptable and God's blessing is never on it. God will take the initiative against this kind of daydreaming by prodding us to action.

DO YOU REALLY LOVE HIM?

"She has done a good work for Me."

MARK 14:6

Have you ever been driven to do something for God not because you felt that it was useful or your duty to do so, or that there was anything in it for you, but simply because you love Him?

There are times when it seems as if God watches to see if we will give Him even small gifts of surrender, just to show how genuine our love is for Him. Once we are totally surrendered to God, He will work through us all the time.

THE DISCIPLINE OF SPIRITUAL PERSEVERANCE

"Be still, and know that I am God."

PSALM 46:10

Perseverance is more than endurance. It is endurance combined with absolute assurance and certainty that what we are looking for is going to happen.

If our hopes seem to be experiencing disappointment right now, it simply means that they are being purified. Every hope or dream of the human mind will be fulfilled if it is noble and of God. But one of the greatest stresses in life is the stress of waiting for God.

THE DETERMINATION TO SERVE

"The Son of Man did not come to be served, but to serve."
MATTHEW 20:28

I f our devotion is to the cause of humanity, we will be quickly defeated and brokenhearted, since we will often be confronted with a great deal of ingratitude from other people. But if we are motivated by our love for God, no amount of ingratitude will be able to hinder us from serving one another.

Once we realize that Jesus has served us even to the depths of our meagerness, selfishness, and sin, nothing we encounter from others will be able to exhaust our determination to serve others for His sake.

THE DELIGHT OF SACRIFICE

I will very gladly spend and be spent for your souls.

2 CORINTHIANS 12:15

We have no right in Christian service to be guided by our own interests and desires. In fact, this is one of the greatest tests of our relationship with Jesus Christ. The delight of sacrifice is that I lay down my life for my Friend, Jesus. I don't throw my life away, but I willingly and deliberately lay it down for Him and His interests in other people.

If we are totally surrendered to Him, we have no goals of our own to serve.

THE DESTITUTION OF SERVICE

*Though the more abundantly I love you,
the less I am loved.*

2 CORINTHIANS 12:15

Jesus Christ's idea is that we serve Him by being the servants of others. The real test of a saint is not one's willingness to preach the gospel, but one's willingness to do something like washing the disciples' feet—that is, being willing to do those things that seem unimportant in human estimation but count as everything to God.

Our Misgivings about Jesus

"Sir, You have nothing to draw with."

John 4:11

I f we are honest, we will admit that we never have misgivings or doubts about ourselves, because we know exactly what we are capable or incapable of doing. But we do have misgivings about Jesus.

If I detect misgivings in myself, I should confess them—"Lord, I have had misgivings about You. I have not believed in Your abilities but only in my own. And I have not believed in Your almighty power apart from my finite understanding of it."

THE IMPOVERISHED MINISTRY OF JESUS

"Where then do You get that living water?"

JOHN 4:11

Have you been limiting, or impoverishing, the ministry of Jesus to the point that He is unable to work in your life? We limit the Holy One of Israel by remembering only what we have allowed Him to do for us in the past. We impoverish and weaken His ministry in us the moment we forget He is almighty. The impoverishment is in us, not in Him. The well of your incompleteness runs deep, but make the effort to look away from yourself and to look toward Him.

"Do You Now Believe?"

"By this we believe that You came forth from God."
Jesus answered them, "Do you now believe?"

JOHN 16:30–31

I f we do something simply out of a sense of duty, we are trying to live up to a standard that competes with Jesus Christ. We have put our sense of duty on the throne of our life instead of enthroning the resurrection life of Jesus. When we do something out of a sense of duty, it is easy to explain the reasons for our actions to others. But when we do something out of obedience to the Lord, there can be no other explanation—just obedience.

WHAT DO YOU WANT THE LORD TO DO FOR YOU?

"Lord, that I may receive my sight."

LUKE 18:41

Is there something in your life that disturbs you? Be persistent with your disturbance until you get face-to-face with the Lord Himself. Don't deify common sense. To sit calmly by, instead of creating a disturbance, serves only to deify our common sense. When Jesus asks what we want Him to do for us about the incredible problem that is confronting us, remember that He doesn't work in commonsense ways but only in supernatural ways.

THE PIERCING QUESTION

"Do you love Me?"

JOHN 21:17

P eter's response to this piercing question is considerably different from the bold defiance he exhibited only a few days before when he declared, "Even if I have to die with You, I will not deny You!" Our natural individuality, or our natural self, boldly speaks out and declares its feelings. But the true love within our inner spiritual self can be discovered only by experiencing the hurt of this question of Jesus Christ.

HAVE YOU FELT THE PAIN INFLICTED BY THE LORD?

He said to him the third time, "Do you love Me?"

JOHN 21:17

Have you ever felt the pain, inflicted by the Lord, at the very center of your being, deep down in the most sensitive area of your life? The devil never inflicts pain there, and neither can sin nor human emotions. Nothing can cut through to that part of our being but the Word of God. Our Lord never asks questions until the perfect time. Then we will realize that we do love Him far more deeply than our words can ever say.

His Commission to Us

"Feed My sheep."

JOHN 21:17

This is love in the making. The love of God is not created—it is His nature. When we receive the life of Christ through the Holy Spirit, He unites us with God so that His love is demonstrated in us. The goal of the indwelling Holy Spirit is not just to unite us with God, but to do it in such a way that we will be one with the Father in exactly the same way Jesus is.

IS THIS TRUE OF ME?

But none of these things move me;
nor do I count my life dear to myself.

ACTS 20:24

It is easier to serve or work for God without a vision and without a call, because then you are not bothered by what He requires. But once you receive a commission from Jesus Christ, the memory of what God asks of you will always be there to prod you on to do His will. You will no longer be able to work for Him on the basis of common sense. Never consider whether or not you are of use—you are His.

IS HE REALLY MY LORD?

So that I may finish my race with joy, and the ministry which I received from the Lord Jesus.

ACTS 20:24

Have you received a ministry from the Lord? If so, you must be faithful to it—to consider your life valuable only for the purpose of fulfilling that ministry. Think how satisfying it will be to hear Him say to you, "Well done, good and faithful servant" (Matthew 25:21). We each have to find a niche in life, and spiritually we find it when we receive a ministry from the Lord. To do this we must have close fellowship with Jesus.

TAKING THE NEXT STEP

In much patience, in tribulations, in needs, in distresses. . .
2 CORINTHIANS 6:4

Every Christian must experience the essence of the incarnation by bringing the next step down into flesh-and-blood reality and by working it out with his hands. The thing that really testifies for God and for the people of God in the long run is steady perseverance. Ask God to keep the eyes of your spirit open to the risen Christ, and it will be impossible for drudgery to discourage you. Never allow yourself to think that some tasks are beneath your dignity or too insignificant for you to do.

THE SOURCE OF ABUNDANT JOY

Yet in all these things we are more than conquerors through Him who loved us.

ROMANS 8:37

The things we try to avoid and fight against—tribulation, suffering, and persecution—are the very things that produce abundant joy in us. A saint doesn't know the joy of the Lord in spite of tribulation but *because* of it.

The undiminished radiance, which is the result of abundant joy, is not built on anything passing but on the love of God that nothing can change.

THE SURRENDERED LIFE

I have been crucified with Christ.

GALATIANS 2:20

To become one with Jesus Christ, a person must be willing to surrender his whole way of looking at things. Being born again means that we must first be willing to let go before we can grasp something else.

If you are faced with the question of whether or not to surrender, make a determination to go on through the crisis, surrendering all that you have and all that you are to Him. And God will then equip you to do all that He requires of you.

TURNING BACK OR WALKING WITH JESUS?

"Do you also want to go away?"

JOHN 6:67

Many people today are pouring their lives out and working for Jesus Christ but are not really walking with Him. One thing God constantly requires of us is a oneness with Jesus Christ. All that is required is to live a natural life of absolute dependence on Jesus Christ. Never try to live your life with God in any other way than His way. And His way means absolute devotion to Him. Showing no concern for the uncertainties that lie ahead is the secret of walking with Jesus.

BEING AN EXAMPLE
OF HIS MESSAGE

Preach the word!

2 TIMOTHY 4:2

We are not saved only to be instruments for God, but to be His sons and daughters. As His disciples, our lives must be a holy example of the reality of our message. Even the natural heart of the unsaved will serve if called upon to do so, but it takes a heart broken by conviction of sin, baptized by the Holy Spirit, and crushed into submission to God's purpose to make a person's life a holy example of God's message.

OBEDIENCE TO THE "HEAVENLY VISION"

"I was not disobedient to the heavenly vision."

ACTS 26:19

The only way to be obedient to the "heavenly vision" is to give our utmost for His highest—our best for His glory. This can be accomplished only when we make a determination to continually remember God's vision. But the acid test is obedience to the vision in the details of our everyday life—sixty seconds out of every minute, and sixty minutes out of every hour, not just during times of personal prayer or public meetings.

TOTAL SURRENDER

Then Peter began to say to Him,
"See, we have left all and followed You."

MARK 10:28

True surrender will always go beyond natural devotion. If we will only give up, God will surrender Himself to embrace all those around us and will meet their needs, which were created by our surrender. Beware of stopping anywhere short of total surrender to God. Most of us have only a vision of what this really means but have never truly experienced it.

GOD'S TOTAL SURRENDER TO US

God so loved the world that He gave...

JOHN 3:16

If we are truly surrendered, we will never be aware of our own efforts to remain surrendered. Beware of talking about surrender if you know nothing about it. In fact, you will never know anything about it until you understand that John 3:16 means that God completely and absolutely gave Himself to us. In our surrender, we must give ourselves to God in the same way He gave Himself for us—totally, unconditionally, and without reservation.

YIELDING

You are that one's slaves whom you obey.

ROMANS 6:16

The first thing I must be willing to admit when I begin to examine what controls and dominates me is that I am the one responsible for having yielded myself to whatever it may be. If I am a slave to myself, I am to blame because somewhere in the past I yielded to myself. Likewise, if I obey God, I do so because at some point in my life I yielded myself to Him.

Yielding to Jesus will break every kind of slavery in any person's life.

THE DISCIPLINE OF DISMAY

And as they followed they were afraid.

MARK 10:32

The discipline of dismay is an essential lesson that a disciple must learn. The danger is that we tend to look back on our times of obedience and on our past sacrifices to God in an effort to keep our enthusiasm for Him strong. But when the darkness of dismay comes, endure until it is over, because out of it will come the ability to follow Jesus truly, which brings inexpressibly wonderful joy.

THE MASTER WILL JUDGE

For we must all appear before the judgment seat of Christ.

2 CORINTHIANS 5:10

P aul says that we must all, preachers and other people alike, "appear before the judgment seat of Christ." But if you will learn here and now to live under the scrutiny of Christ's pure light, your final judgment will bring you only delight in seeing the work God has done in you. Live constantly, reminding yourself of the judgment seat of Christ, and walk in the knowledge of the holiness He has given you.

THE SERVANT'S PRIMARY GOAL

Therefore we make it our aim. . .to be well pleasing to Him.

2 CORINTHIANS 5:9

Any goal we have that diverts us even to the slightest degree from the central goal of being "approved to God" (2 Timothy 2:15) may result in our rejection from further service for Him.

I must learn to relate everything to the primary goal, maintaining it without interruption. My worth to God publicly is measured by what I really am in my private life. Is my primary goal in life to please Him and to be acceptable to Him, or is it something less, no matter how lofty it may sound?

WILL I BRING MYSELF UP TO THIS LEVEL?

Perfecting holiness in the fear of God. . .

2 CORINTHIANS 7:1

Christ never spoke of His right to Himself but always maintained an inner vigilance to submit His spirit continually to His Father. I also have the responsibility to keep my spirit in agreement with His Spirit. And when I do, Jesus gradually lifts me up to the level where He lived— a level of perfect submission to His Father's will. Is God having His way with me, and are people beginning to see God in my life more and more?

ABRAHAM'S LIFE OF FAITH

He went out, not knowing where he was going.

HEBREWS 11:8

In the Old Testament, a person's relationship with God was seen by the degree of separation in that person's life. This separation is exhibited in the life of Abraham by his separation from his country and his family.

Living a life of faith means never knowing where you are being led. But it does mean loving and knowing the One who is leading. It is literally a life of *faith*, not of understanding and reason—a life of knowing Him who calls us to go.

FRIENDSHIP WITH GOD

"Shall I hide from Abraham what I am doing?"

GENESIS 18:17

Genesis 18 brings out the delight of true friendship with God. This friendship means being so intimately in touch with God that you never even need to ask Him to show you His will. It is evidence of a level of intimacy which confirms that you are nearing the final stage of your discipline in the life of faith. When you have a right-standing relationship with God, you have a life of freedom, liberty, and delight; you *are* God's will.

IDENTIFIED OR SIMPLY INTERESTED?

I have been crucified with Christ.

GALATIANS 2:20

The inescapable spiritual need each of us has is the need to sign the death certificate of our sin nature. I must take my emotional opinions and intellectual beliefs and be willing to turn them into a moral verdict against the nature of sin; that is, against any claim I have to my right to myself. Once I reach this moral decision and act on it, all that Christ accomplished *for* me on the Cross is accomplished *in* me.

THE BURNING HEART

"Did not our heart burn within us?"

LUKE 24:32

We need to learn this secret of the burning heart. Suddenly Jesus appears to us, fires are set ablaze, and we are given wonderful visions; but then we must learn to maintain the secret of the burning heart—a heart that can go through anything. It is the simple, dreary day, with its commonplace duties and people, that smothers the burning heart—unless we have learned the secret of abiding in Jesus.

AM I CARNALLY MINDED?

For where there are envy, strife. . .are you not carnal?

1 CORINTHIANS 3:3

Are you quarrelsome and easily upset over small things? Do you think that no one who is a Christian is ever like that? Paul said they are, and he connected these attitudes with carnality.

What is the proof that carnality has gone? Never deceive yourself; when carnality is gone you will know it—it is the most real thing you can imagine.

DECREASING FOR HIS PURPOSE

"He must increase, but I must decrease."

JOHN 3:30

When you see a person who is close to grasping the claims of Jesus Christ, you know that your influence has been used in the right direction. And when you begin to see that person in the middle of a difficult and painful struggle, don't try to prevent it, but pray that his difficulty will grow even ten times stronger, until no power on earth or in hell could hold him away from Jesus Christ.

MAINTAINING THE PROPER RELATIONSHIP

The friend of the bridegroom. . .

JOHN 3:29

To maintain friendship and faithfulness to the Bridegroom, we have to be more careful to have the moral and vital relationship to Him above everything else, including obedience. Sometimes there is nothing to obey and our only task is to maintain a vital connection with Jesus Christ, seeing that nothing interferes with it. Only occasionally is it a matter of obedience. At those times when a crisis arises, we have to find out what God's will is.

SPIRITUAL VISION THROUGH PERSONAL PURITY

"Blessed are the pure in heart, for they shall see God."
MATTHEW 5:8

Purity is not innocence—it is much more than that. Purity is the result of continued spiritual harmony with God. We have to grow in purity. Our life with God may be right and our inner purity unblemished, yet occasionally our outer life may become spotted and stained. God intentionally does not protect us from this possibility, because this is the way we recognize the necessity of maintaining our spiritual vision through personal purity.

SPIRITUAL VISION THROUGH PERSONAL CHARACTER

"Come up here, and I will show you things."
REVELATION 4:1

A higher state of mind and spiritual vision can only be achieved through the higher practice of personal character. If you live up to the highest and best that you know in the outer level of your life, God will continually say to you, "Friend, come up even higher." When God elevates you by His grace into heavenly places, you find a vast plateau where you can move about with ease.

ISN'T THERE SOME MISUNDERSTANDING?

"Let us go to Judea again." The disciples said to Him. . .
"Are You going there again?"

JOHN 11:7–8

Just because I don't understand what Jesus Christ says, I have no right to determine that He must be mistaken in what He says. That is a dangerous view, and it is never right to think that my obedience to God's directive will bring dishonor to Jesus. The only thing that will bring dishonor is not obeying Him. To put my view of His honor ahead of what He is plainly guiding me to do is never right.

OUR LORD'S SURPRISE VISITS

"Therefore you also be ready."

LUKE 12:40

Jesus rarely comes where we expect Him; He appears where we least expect Him, and always in the most illogical situations. The only way a servant can remain true to God is to be ready for the Lord's surprise visits. This readiness will not be brought about by service but through intense spiritual reality, expecting Jesus Christ at every turn. This sense of expectation will give our life the attitude of childlike wonder He wants it to have.

HOLINESS OR HARDNESS TOWARD GOD?

He. . .wondered that there was no intercessor.

ISAIAH 59:16

A re we worshipping God in a way that will raise us up to where we can take hold of Him, having such intimate contact with Him that we know His mind about the ones for whom we pray? Are we living in a holy relationship with God, or have we become hard and dogmatic?

Be a person who worships God and lives in a holy relationship with Him. Get involved in the real work of intercession.

HEEDFULNESS OR HYPOCRISY IN OURSELVES?

If anyone sees his brother sinning a sin which does not lead to death, he will ask, and He will give him life for those who commit sin not leading to death.

1 JOHN 5:16

I f we are not heedful and pay no attention to the way the Spirit of God works in us, we will become spiritual hypocrites. We see other people failing, and then we take our discernment and turn it into ridicule and criticism, instead of turning it into intercession. Be careful that you don't become a hypocrite by spending all your time trying to get others right with God before you worship Him yourself.

HELPFUL OR HEARTLESS
TOWARD OTHERS?

The Spirit. . .makes intercession for the saints. . . .
It is Christ. . .who also makes intercession for us.

ROMANS 8:27, 34

Beware of getting ahead of God by your very desire to do His will. God continually introduces us to people in whom we have no interest, and the natural tendency is to be heartless toward them. We give them a quick verse of scripture, like jabbing them with a spear, or leave them with a hurried, uncaring word of counsel before we go. Are our lives in the proper place so that we may participate in the intercession of our Lord and the Holy Spirit?

THE GLORY THAT'S UNSURPASSED

"The Lord. . .has sent me that you may receive your sight."

ACTS 9:17

We must learn to maintain a strong degree of character in our lives, even to the level that has been revealed in our vision of Jesus Christ.

The lasting characteristic of a spiritual man is the ability to understand correctly the meaning of the Lord Jesus Christ in his life, and the ability to explain the purposes of God to others. The overruling passion of his life is Jesus Christ.

"IF YOU HAD KNOWN!"

*"If you had known. . .in this your day,
the things that make for your peace!
But now they are hidden from your eyes."*

LUKE 19:42

God never again opens the doors that have been closed. He opens other doors, but He reminds us that there are doors which we have shut. Let your memory have its way with you. It is a minister of God bringing its rebuke and sorrow to you. God will turn what might have been into a wonderful lesson of growth for the future.

THE WAY TO PERMANENT FAITH

Indeed the hour is coming. . .that you will be scattered.

JOHN 16:32

We will be scattered, not into service but into the emptiness of our lives where we will see ruin and barrenness, to know what internal death to God's blessings means. Until we have been through that experience, our faith is sustained only by feelings and by blessings. But once we get there, no matter where God may place us or what inner emptiness we experience, we can praise God that all is well. That is what is meant by faith being exercised in the realities of life.

HIS AGONY AND OUR ACCESS

Then Jesus came with them to a place called Gethsemane,
and said to the disciples. . .
"Stay here and watch with Me."

MATTHEW 26:36, 38

The agony in Gethsemane was the agony of the Son of God in fulfilling His destiny as the Savior of the world. The veil is pulled back here to reveal all that it cost Him to make it possible for us to become sons of God. His agony was the basis for the simplicity of our salvation. Because of what the Son of Man went through, every human being has been provided with a way of access into the very presence of God.

THE COLLISION OF GOD AND SIN

Who Himself bore our sins in His own body on the tree. . .

1 PETER 2:24

The heart of salvation is the Cross of Christ. The reason salvation is so easy to obtain is that it cost God so much. The Cross was the place where God and sinful man merged with a tremendous collision and where the way to life was opened. But all the cost and pain of the collision was absorbed by the heart of God.

WHY WE LACK UNDERSTANDING

*He commanded them that they
should tell no one the things they had seen,
till the Son of Man had risen from the dead.*

MARK 9:9

When you grow and develop the right condition inwardly, the words Jesus spoke become so clear that you are amazed you did not grasp them before. In fact, you were not able to understand them before because you had not yet developed the proper spiritual condition to deal with them.

God cannot reveal anything to us if we don't have His Spirit. But our insensible thinking will end immediately once His resurrection life has its way with us.

HIS RESURRECTION DESTINY

*"Ought not the Christ to have suffered these things
and to enter into His glory?"*

LUKE 24:26

Christ's resurrection destiny—His fore-ordained purpose—was to bring "many sons to glory" (Hebrews 2:10). The fulfilling of His destiny gives Him the right to make us sons and daughters of God. We never have exactly the same relationship to God that the Son of God has, but we are brought by the Son into the relation of sonship.

Thank God for the glorious and majestic truth that His Spirit can work the very nature of Jesus into us, if we will only obey Him.

HAVE YOU SEEN JESUS?

After that, He appeared in another form to two of them.

MARK 16:12

Being saved and seeing Jesus are not the same thing. Many people who have never seen Jesus have received and share in God's grace. But once you have seen Him, you can never be the same. Other things will not have the appeal they did before.

Have you seen Jesus? If so, you will want others to see Him, too. When you see Him, you must tell, even if they don't believe.

COMPLETE AND EFFECTIVE
DECISION ABOUT SIN

Knowing this, that our old man was crucified with Him,
that the body of sin might be done away with,
that we should no longer be slaves of sin.

ROMANS 6:6

Have you made the following decision about sin—that it must be completely killed in you? It takes a long time to come to the point of making this complete and effective decision about sin. It is, however, the greatest moment in your life once you decide that sin must die in you—not simply be restrained, suppressed, or counteracted, but crucified—just as Jesus Christ died for the sin of the world.

COMPLETE AND EFFECTIVE DIVINITY

*For if we have been united together
in the likeness of His death, certainly
we also shall be in the likeness of His resurrection.*

ROMANS 6:5

After the decision to be identified with Jesus in His death has been made, the resurrection life of Jesus penetrates every bit of my human nature. It takes the omnipotence of God—His complete and effective divinity—to live the life of the Son of God in human flesh. The Holy Spirit cannot be accepted as a guest in merely one room of the house—He invades all of it. My part is to walk in the light and to obey all that He reveals to me.

COMPLETE AND EFFECTIVE DOMINION

Death no longer has dominion over Him. . . .
But the life that He lives, He lives to God. Likewise you also,
reckon yourselves to be dead indeed to sin,
but alive to God in Christ Jesus our Lord.

ROMANS 6:9–11

Even the weakest saint can experience the power of the deity of the Son of God when he is willing to "let go." But any effort to "hang on" to the least bit of our own power will only diminish the life of Jesus in us. We have to keep letting go, and slowly but surely the great, full life of God will invade us, penetrating every part. Then Jesus will have complete and effective dominion in us, and people will take notice that we have been with Him.

WHAT TO DO WHEN YOUR BURDEN IS OVERWHELMING

Cast your burden on the LORD.

PSALM 55:22

You have been bearing it all, but you need to deliberately place one end on God's shoulder. Commit to God whatever burden He has placed on you. Don't just cast it aside, but put it over onto Him and place yourself there with it. You will see that your burden is then lightened by the sense of companionship. But you should never try to separate yourself from your burden.

INNER INVINCIBILITY

"Take My yoke upon you and learn from Me."

MATTHEW 11:29

The burden that God places on us squeezes the grapes in our lives and produces the wine, but most of us see only the wine and not the burden. No power on earth or in hell can conquer the Spirit of God living within the human spirit; it creates an inner invincibility.

If your life is producing only a whine, instead of the wine, then ruthlessly kick it out. It is definitely a crime for a Christian to be weak in God's strength.

THE FAILURE TO PAY
CLOSE ATTENTION

But the high places were not removed from Israel.
Nevertheless the heart of Asa was loyal all his days.

2 CHRONICLES 15:17

Are there some things regarding your physical or intellectual life to which you have been paying no attention at all? You no more need a day off from spiritual concentration on matters in your life than your heart needs a day off from beating. As you cannot take a day off morally and remain moral, neither can you take a day off spiritually and remain spiritual. God wants you to be entirely His, and it requires paying close attention to keep yourself fit.

CAN YOU COME DOWN FROM THE MOUNTAIN?

"While you have the light, believe in the light."

JOHN 12:36

We all have moments when we feel better than ever before, and we say, "I feel fit for anything; if only I could always be like this!" We are not meant to be. Those moments are moments of insight that we have to live up to even when we do not feel like it. Many of us are no good for the everyday world when we are not on the mountaintop. Yet we must bring our everyday life up to the standard revealed to us on the mountaintop when we were there.

ALL OR NOTHING?

Now when Simon Peter heard that it was the Lord,
he put on his outer garment. . .and plunged into the sea.

JOHN 21:7

Have you ever had a crisis in your life in which you deliberately, earnestly, and recklessly abandoned everything? It is a crisis of the will. You may come to that point many times externally, but it will amount to nothing. The true deep crisis of abandonment, or total surrender, is reached internally, not externally.

Have you deliberately committed your will to Jesus Christ? Make the determination to surrender your will.

READINESS

God called to him. . .and he said, "Here I am."

EXODUS 3:4

Readiness for God means that we are prepared to do the smallest thing or the largest thing—it makes no difference. It means we have no choice in what we want to do, but that whatever God's plans may be, we are there and ready. Whenever any duty presents itself, we hear God's voice as our Lord heard His Father's voice, and we are ready for it with the total readiness of our love for Him.

A ready person never needs to *get* ready—he *is* ready.

BEWARE OF THE LEAST LIKELY TEMPTATION

For Joab had defected to Adonijah,
though he had not defected to Absalom.

1 KINGS 2:28

Be alert about the things that may appear to be the least likely to tempt you. Beware of thinking that the areas of your life where you have experienced victory in the past are now the least likely to cause you to stumble and fall.

It is in the aftermath of a great spiritual event that the least likely things begin to have an effect. They may not be forceful and dominant, but they are there. And if you are not careful to be forewarned, they will trip you.

CAN A SAINT FALSELY ACCUSE GOD?

*For all the promises of God in Him are Yes,
and in Him Amen.*

2 CORINTHIANS 1:20

We must never measure our spiritual capacity on the basis of our education or our intellect; our capacity in spiritual things is measured on the basis of the promises of God. Never allow the limitation of your own natural ability to enter into the matter. If we have received the Holy Spirit, God expects the work of the Holy Spirit to be exhibited in us.

Never forget that our capacity and capability in spiritual matters is measured by, and based on, the promises of God.

DON'T HURT THE LORD

*"Have I been with you so long,
and yet you have not known Me, Philip?"*

JOHN 14:9

It is highly probable that we are hurting [Jesus] by what we ask—"Lord, show us the Father. . ." (14:8). We look for God to exhibit Himself *to* His children, but God only exhibits Himself *in* His children.

I have to get to the point of the absolute and unquestionable relationship that takes everything exactly as it comes from Him. God never guides us at some time in the future, but always here and now. Realize that the Lord is here *now*, and the freedom you receive is immediate.

THE LIGHT THAT NEVER FAILS

We all, with unveiled face, beholding. . .
the glory of the Lord. . .

2 CORINTHIANS 3:18

A servant of God must stand so very much alone that he never realizes he is alone. In the early stages of the Christian life, disappointments will come—people who used to be lights will flicker out, and those who used to stand with us will turn away. We must build our faith not on fading lights but on the Light that never fails.

The secret of the servant's life is that he stays in tune with God all the time.

DO YOU WORSHIP THE WORK?

God's fellow workers. . .

1 CORINTHIANS 3:9

Beware of any work for God that causes or allows you to avoid concentrating on Him. A great number of Christian workers worship their work. The only concern should be their concentration on God.

We have no right to decide where we should be placed, or to have preconceived ideas as to what God is preparing us to do. God engineers everything; and wherever He places us, our one supreme goal should be to pour out our lives in wholehearted devotion to Him in that particular work.

THE WARNING AGAINST DESIRING SPIRITUAL SUCCESS

*"Nevertheless do not rejoice in this,
that the spirits are subject to you. . ."*

LUKE 10:20

Worldliness is not the trap that most endangers us as Christian workers; nor is it sin. The trap we fall into is extravagantly desiring spiritual success; that is, success measured by, and patterned after, the form set by this religious age in which we now live. Never seek after anything other than the approval of God. One life totally devoted to God is of more value to Him than one hundred lives which have been simply awakened by His Spirit.

"READY IN SEASON"

Be ready in season and out of season.

2 TIMOTHY 4:2

Many of us suffer from the unbalanced tendency to "be ready" only "out of season." If we do only what we feel inclined to do, some of us would never do anything. There are some people who are totally unemployable in the spiritual realm. They are spiritually feeble and weak, and they refuse to do anything unless they are supernaturally inspired. The proof that our relationship is right with God is that we do our best whether we feel inspired or not.

THE SUPREME CLIMB

*"Take now your son. . .and offer him
there as a burnt offering on one of
the mountains of which I shall tell you."*

GENESIS 22:2

The great lesson to be learned from Abraham's faith in God is that he was prepared to do anything for God. He was there to obey God, no matter what contrary belief of his might be violated by his obedience. If you will remain true to God, God will lead you directly through every barrier and right into the inner chamber of the knowledge of Himself. Don't ask God to test you. Abraham did not make any such statement—he simply remained true to God, and God purified his faith.

WHAT DO YOU WANT?

"Do you seek great things for yourself?"

JEREMIAH 45:5

Are you seeking great things for yourself instead of seeking to be a great person? God wants you to be in a much closer relationship with Himself than simply receiving His gifts—He wants you to get to know Him. Even some large thing we want is only incidental; it comes and it goes. But God never gives us anything incidental. There is nothing easier than getting into the right relationship with God.

WHAT YOU WILL GET

*"I will give your life to you as a prize in all places,
wherever you go."*

JEREMIAH 45:5

Are you prepared to let God take you into total oneness with Himself, paying no more attention to what you call the great things of life? Are you prepared to surrender totally and let go? Abandonment means to refuse yourself the luxury of asking any questions. If you totally abandon yourself to God, He immediately says to you, "I will give your life to you as a prize."

GRACIOUS UNCERTAINTY

It has not yet been revealed what we shall be.

1 JOHN 3:2

Certainty is the mark of the commonsense life—gracious uncertainty is the mark of the spiritual life. To be certain of God means that we are uncertain in all our ways, not knowing what tomorrow may bring. We are uncertain of the next step, but we are certain of God. As soon as we abandon ourselves to God and do the task He has placed closest to us, He begins to fill our lives with surprises.

SPONTANEOUS LOVE

Love suffers long and is kind.

1 CORINTHIANS 13:4

Love is not premeditated—it is spontaneous; that is, it bursts forth in extraordinary ways.

If we try to prove to God how much we love Him, it is a sure sign that we really don't love Him. The evidence of our love for Him is the absolute spontaneity of our love, which flows naturally from His nature within us. The life of God exhibits itself in this spontaneous way because the fountains of His love are in the Holy Spirit.

FAITH—NOT EMOTION

For we walk by faith, not by sight.

2 CORINTHIANS 5:7

A self-assured saint is of no value to God. He is abnormal, unfit for daily life, and completely unlike God. We are here, not as immature angels, but as men and women, to do the work of this world. And we are to do it with an infinitely greater power to withstand the struggle because we have been born from above.

What God wants us to do is to "walk by faith." We must never consider our moments of inspiration as the standard way of life—our work is our standard.

THE PATIENCE TO WAIT FOR THE VISION

Though it tarries, wait for it.

HABAKKUK 2:3

Patience is not the same as indifference; patience conveys the idea of someone who is tremendously strong and able to withstand all assaults. Having the vision of God is the source of patience because it gives us God's true and proper inspiration. A person who has the vision of God is not devoted to a cause or to any particular issue— he is devoted to God Himself.

VITAL INTERCESSION

*Praying always with all prayer
and supplication in the Spirit. . .*

EPHESIANS 6:18

I t is impossible for us to have living and vital intercession unless we are perfectly and completely sure of God. And the greatest destroyer of that confident relationship to God is our own personal sympathy and preconceived bias. Identification with God is the key to intercession, and whenever we stop being identified with Him, it is because of our sympathy with others, not because of sin. It is sympathy with ourselves or with others that makes us say, "I will not allow that thing to happen." And instantly we are out of that vital connection with God.

VICARIOUS INTERCESSION

*Therefore, brethren, having boldness to enter
the Holiest by the blood of Jesus. . .*

HEBREWS 10:19

Beware of thinking that intercession means bringing our own personal sympathies and concerns into the presence of God and then demanding that He do whatever we ask. Our ability to approach God is due entirely to the vicarious, or substitutionary, identification of our Lord with sin. We have "boldness to enter the Holiest *by the blood of Jesus.*" Vicarious intercession means that we deliberately substitute God's interests in others for our natural sympathy with them.

JUDGMENT AND THE LOVE OF GOD

*For the time has come for judgment
to begin at the house of God.*

I PETER 4:17

I n the teachings of Jesus Christ the element of
judgment is always brought out—it is the sign
of the love of God. Never sympathize with someone
who finds it difficult to get to God; God is not to
blame. It is not for us to figure out the reason for
the difficulty, but only to present the truth of God
so that the Spirit of God will reveal what is wrong.
When the truth is preached, the Spirit of God
brings each person face-to-face with God Himself.

LIBERTY AND THE STANDARDS OF JESUS

Stand fast therefore in the liberty by which Christ has made us free.

GALATIANS 5:1

We are not asked to believe the Bible but to believe the One whom the Bible reveals. We are called to present liberty for the conscience of others, not to bring them liberty for their thoughts and opinions. And if we ourselves are free with the liberty of Christ, others will be brought into that same liberty—the liberty that comes from realizing the absolute control and authority of Jesus Christ.

BUILDING FOR ETERNITY

*"For which of you, intending to build a tower,
does not sit down first and count the cost,
whether he has enough to finish it?"*

LUKE 14:28

The only men and women our Lord will use in His building enterprises are those who love Him personally, passionately, and with great devotion—those who have a love for Him that goes far beyond any of the closest relationships on earth. When God inspects us with His searching and refining fire, will He detect that we have built enterprises of our own on the foundation of Jesus?

THE FAITH TO PERSEVERE

Because you have kept My command to persevere. . .
REVELATION 3:10

Perseverance means more than endurance—
more than simply holding on until the end.
Entrust yourself to God's hands. Is there something
in your life for which you need perseverance right
now? Maintain your intimate relationship with
Jesus Christ through the perseverance of faith.
Proclaim as Job did, "Though He slay me, yet will
I trust Him" (Job 13:15).

Even though you cannot see Him right now and
cannot understand what He is doing, you know *Him.*

REACHING BEYOND OUR GRASP

Where there is no revelation, the people cast off restraint.

PROVERBS 29:18

Once we lose sight of God, we begin to be reckless. We simply begin to act on our own initiative. If we are doing things solely on our own initiative without expecting God to come in, we are on a downward path. We have lost the vision. Is our attitude today an attitude that flows from our vision of God? Are we expecting God to do greater things than He has ever done before? Is there a freshness and a vitality in our spiritual outlook?

TAKE THE INITIATIVE

Add to your faith virtue, to virtue knowledge.

2 PETER 1:5

Stop hesitating—take the first step. Be determined to act immediately in faith on what God says to you, and never reconsider or change your initial decisions. If you hesitate when God tells you to do something, you are being careless, spurning the grace in which you stand. Take the initiative yourself, make a decision of your will right now, and make it impossible to go back. Burn your bridges behind you, saying, "I *will* write that letter," or "I *will* pay that debt"; and then do it!

"LOVE ONE ANOTHER"

Add to your. . .brotherly kindness love.

2 PETER 1:5, 7

The Holy Spirit reveals to me that God loved me not because I was lovable, but because it was His nature to do so. Now He commands me to show the same love to others. He is saying, "I will bring a number of people around you whom you cannot respect, but you must exhibit My love to them, just as I have exhibited it to you." This kind of love is not a patronizing love for the unlovable—it is His love, and it will not be evidenced in us overnight.

THE HABIT OF HAVING
NO HABITS

For if these things are yours and abound,
you will be neither barren nor unfruitful.

2 PETER 1:8

The right thing to do with godly habits is to immerse them in the life of the Lord until they become such a spontaneous expression of our lives that we are no longer aware of them. Love means that there are no visible habits—that your habits are so immersed in the Lord that you practice them without realizing it. Is there someplace where you are not at home with God? Then allow God to work through whatever that particular circumstance may be until you increase in Him, adding His qualities.

THE HABIT OF KEEPING A CLEAR CONSCIENCE

Always strive to have a conscience without offense toward God and men.

ACTS 24:16

Conscience is that ability within me that attaches itself to the highest standard I know and then continually reminds me of what that standard demands I do. If I am in the habit of continually holding God's standard in front of me, my conscience will always direct me to God's perfect law and indicate what I should do. The question is, will I obey? I have to make an effort to keep my conscience so sensitive that I can live without any offense toward anyone.

THE HABIT OF ENJOYING ADVERSITY

That the life of Jesus also may be manifested in our mortal flesh. . .

2 CORINTHIANS 4:11

It is adversity that makes us exhibit [God's] life in our mortal flesh. Is my life exhibiting the essence of the sweetness of the Son of God? The only thing that will enable me to enjoy adversity is the acute sense of eagerness of allowing the life of the Son of God to evidence itself in me. No matter how difficult something may be, I must say, "Lord, I am delighted to obey You in this."

THE HABIT OF RISING TO THE OCCASION

That you may know what is the hope of His calling. . .

EPHESIANS 1:18

Remember that you have been saved so that the life of Jesus may be manifested in your body. Direct the total energy of your powers so that you may achieve everything your election as a child of God provides; rise every time to whatever occasion may come your way.

You did not do anything to achieve your salvation, but you must do something to exhibit it. You must "work *out* your own salvation" which God has worked in you already.

THE HABIT OF RECOGNIZING GOD'S PROVISION

Partakers of the divine nature. . .

2 PETER 1:4

All of Almighty God is ours in the Lord Jesus! And He will reach to the last grain of sand and the remotest star to bless us if we will only obey Him. Does it really matter that our circumstances are difficult? Why shouldn't they be!

Learn to lavish the grace of God on others, generously giving of yourself. Be marked and identified with God's nature, and His blessing will flow through you all the time.

HIS ASCENSION AND OUR ACCESS

Now it came to pass, while He blessed them,
that He was parted from them and carried up into heaven.

LUKE 24:51

The ascension is the complete fulfillment of the transfiguration. Our Lord returned to His original glory, but not simply as the Son of God—He returned to His Father as the *Son of Man*, as well. There is now freedom of access for anyone straight to the very throne of God. As the Son of Man, Jesus Christ deliberately limited His omnipotence, omnipresence, and omniscience. But now they are His in absolute, full power. As the Son of Man, Jesus Christ now has all the power at the throne of God. From His ascension forward He is the King of kings and Lord of lords.

LIVING SIMPLY—YET FOCUSED

"Look at the birds of the air. . . .
Consider the lilies of the field."

MATTHEW 6:26, 28

Consider the lilies of the field, how they grow: they neither toil nor spin"—they simply *are*! Our heavenly Father knows our circumstances, and if we will stay focused on Him, instead of our circumstances, we will grow spiritually—just as the "lilies of the field."

If you want to be of use to God, maintain the proper relationship with Jesus Christ by staying focused on Him, and He will make use of you every minute you live.

"OUT OF THE WRECK I RISE"

Who shall separate us from the love of Christ?
ROMANS 8:35

God does not keep His child immune from trouble. It doesn't matter how real or intense the adversities may be; nothing can ever separate him from his relationship to God. Tribulation is never a grand, highly welcomed event; but whatever it may be—whether exhausting, irritating, or simply causing some weakness—it is not able to "separate us from the love of Christ." Never allow tribulations or the "cares of this world" to separate you from remembering that God loves you (Matthew 13:22).

TAKING POSSESSION
OF OUR OWN SOULS

By your patience possess your souls.

LUKE 21:19

Many of us prefer to stay at the entrance to the Christian life instead of going on to create and build our souls in accordance with the new life God has placed within us. We have to pick ourselves up by the back of the neck and shake ourselves; then we will find that we can do what we believed we were unable to do. The problem is simply that we *won't.* The Christian life is one of spiritual courage and determination lived out in our flesh.

HAVING GOD'S
"UNREASONABLE" FAITH

*"But seek first the kingdom of God and His righteousness,
and all these things shall be added to you."*

MATTHEW 6:33

Our Lord pointed out that from His standpoint it is absolutely unreasonable for us to be anxious, worrying about how we will live. Jesus taught that His disciple must make his relationship with God the dominating focus of his life and be cautiously carefree about everything else in comparison to that. Jesus is saying that the greatest concern of life is to place our relationship with God first, and everything else second.

THE EXPLANATION FOR OUR DIFFICULTIES

"That they all may be one, as You, Father, are in Me, and I in You; that they also may be one in Us."

JOHN 17:21

The things we are going through are either making us sweeter, better, and nobler men and women, or they are making us more critical and faultfinding and more insistent on our own way. When we understand God's purpose, we will not become small-minded and cynical. Jesus prayed nothing less for us than absolute oneness with Himself, just as He was one with the Father. Some of us are far from this oneness; yet God will not leave us alone until we *are* one with Him.

OUR CAREFUL UNBELIEF

"Therefore I say to you, do not worry about your life,
what you will eat or what you will drink;
nor about your body, what you will put on."

MATTHEW 6:25

Don't take the pressure of your provision upon yourself. It is not only wrong to worry; it is unbelief. Worrying means we do not believe that God can look after the practical details of our lives, and it is never anything but those details that worry us. The only cure for unbelief is obedience to the Spirit.

THE DELIGHT OF DESPAIR

And when I saw Him, I fell at His feet as dead.

REVELATION 1:17

The delight of despair comes when I delight in knowing that there is something in me which must fall prostrate before God when He reveals Himself to me, and also in knowing that if I am ever to be raised up, it must be by the hand of God. God can do nothing for me until I recognize the limits of what is humanly possible, allowing Him to do the impossible.

THE GOOD OR THE BEST?

*"If you take the left, then I will go to the right;
or, if you go to the right, then I will go to the left."*

GENESIS 13:9

Whenever our *right* becomes the guiding factor of our lives, it dulls our spiritual insight. The greatest enemy of the life of faith in God is not sin but good choices which are not quite good enough. The good is always the enemy of the best.

THINKING OF PRAYER
AS JESUS TAUGHT

Pray without ceasing.

I THESSALONIANS 5:17

J esus never mentioned unanswered prayer. He had the unlimited certainty of knowing that prayer is always answered. Do we have through the Spirit of God that inexpressible certainty that Jesus had about prayer, or do we think of the times when it seemed that God did not answer our prayer? God answers prayer in the best way—not just sometimes but every time.

THE LIFE TO KNOW HIM

*"Tarry in the city of Jerusalem until you are endued
with power from on high."*

LUKE 24:49

The Holy Spirit's influence and power were at
work before Pentecost, but *He* was not here.
Once our Lord was glorified in His ascension, the
Holy Spirit came into the world, and He has been
here ever since. We have to receive the revealed
truth that He is here. The attitude of receiving and
welcoming the Holy Spirit into our lives is to be the
continual attitude of believers. When we receive
the Holy Spirit, we receive reviving life from our
ascended Lord.

UNQUESTIONED REVELATION

"And in that day you will ask Me nothing."

JOHN 16:23

If anything is a mystery to you and is coming between you and God, never look for the explanation in your mind, but look for it in your spirit, your true inner nature—that is where the problem is. Once your inner spiritual nature is willing to submit to the life of Jesus, your understanding will be perfectly clear, and you will come to the place where there is no distance between the Father and you, His child, because the Lord has made you one.

UNTROUBLED RELATIONSHIP

"In that day you will ask in My name. . .
the Father Himself loves you."

JOHN 16:26–27

Just as Jesus stood unblemished and pure in the presence of His Father, we too by the mighty power and effectiveness of the baptism of the Holy Spirit can be lifted into that relationship.

Jesus said that because of His name God will recognize and respond to our prayers. Through the resurrection and ascension power of Jesus, and through the Holy Spirit He has sent, we can be lifted into such a relationship.

"YES—BUT. . . !"

"Lord, I will follow You, but. . ."
LUKE 9:61

If a person is ever going to do anything worthwhile, there will be times when he must risk everything by his leap in the dark. In the spiritual realm, Jesus Christ demands that you risk everything you hold on to or believe through common sense, and leap by faith into what He says. Once you obey, you will immediately find that what He says is as solidly consistent as common sense.

PUT GOD FIRST

Jesus did not commit Himself to them. . .
for He knew what was in man.

JOHN 2:24–25

Our Lord never put His trust in any person. He put His trust in God first. He trusted absolutely in what God's grace could do for others. If I put my trust in human beings first, the end result will be my despair and hopelessness toward everyone. I will become bitter because I have insisted that people be what no person can ever be—absolutely perfect and right. Never trust anything in yourself or in anyone else, except the grace of God.

THE STAGGERING QUESTION

"Son of man, can these bones live?"

EZEKIEL 37:3

Can a sinner be turned into a saint? Can a twisted life be made right? There is only one appropriate answer—"O Lord God, You know" (Ezekiel 37:3). Never forge ahead with your religious common sense and say, "Oh yes, with just a little more Bible reading, devotional time, and prayer, I see how it can be done."

Do I really believe that God will do in me what I cannot do?

ARE YOU OBSESSED BY SOMETHING?

Who is the man that fears the LORD?

PSALM 25:12

Are you obsessed by something? You will probably say, "No, by nothing," but all of us are obsessed by something—usually by ourselves, or, if we are Christians, by our own experience of the Christian life. But the psalmist says that we are to be obsessed by God. The abiding awareness of the Christian life is to be God Himself, not just thoughts about Him. The total being of our life inside and out is to be absolutely obsessed by the presence of God.

"THE SECRET OF THE LORD"

The secret of the LORD is with those who fear Him.

PSALM 25:14

What is the sign of a friend? Is it that he tells you his secret sorrows? No, it is that he tells you his secret joys. Many people will confide their secret sorrows to you, but the final mark of intimacy is when they share their secret joys with you. Have we ever let God tell us any of His joys? Or are we continually telling God our secrets, leaving Him no time to talk to us?

THE NEVER-FORSAKING GOD

For He Himself has said,
"I will never leave you nor forsake you."

HEBREWS 13:5

What line of thinking do my thoughts take? Do I turn to what God says or to my own fears? Am I simply repeating what God says, or am I learning to truly hear Him and then to respond after I have heard what He says? "For He Himself has said, 'I will never leave you nor forsake you.' So we may boldly say: 'The Lord is my helper; I will not fear. What can man do to me?' " (Hebrews 13:5–6).

GOD'S ASSURANCE

He Himself has said. . .so we may boldly say. . .
HEBREWS 13:5-6

I will remember God's words of assurance.
I will be full of courage, like a child who strives
to reach the standard his father has set for him.
The faith of many people begins to falter when
apprehensions enter their thinking, and they forget
the meaning of God's assurance—they forget
to take a deep spiritual breath. The only way to
remove the fear from our lives is to listen to God's
assurance to us.

"WORK OUT" WHAT GOD "WORKS IN" YOU

Work out your own salvation.

PHILIPPIANS 2:12

The will is the essential element in God's creation of human beings. In someone who has been born again, the source of the will is Almighty God. With focused attention and great care, you have to "work out" what God "works in" you—not *work* to accomplish or earn "your own salvation," but *work it out* so you will exhibit the evidence of a life based with determined, unshakable faith on the complete and perfect redemption of the Lord.

THE GREATEST SOURCE
OF POWER

"Whatever you ask in My name, that I will do."

JOHN 14:13

What is the greatest source of power in my life? What ought to exert the greatest power in my life is the atonement of the Lord. It is not on what we spend the greatest amount of time that molds us the most, but whatever exerts the most power over us. We must make a determination to limit and concentrate our desires and interests on the atonement by the Cross of Christ.

WHAT'S NEXT TO DO?

"If you know these things, blessed are you if you do them."
JOHN 13:17

If you yourself do not cut the lines that tie you to the dock, God will have to use a storm to sever them and to send you out to sea. Put everything in your life afloat upon God, going out to sea on the great swelling tide of His purpose, and your eyes will be opened. You have to get out past the harbor into the great depths of God, and begin to know things for yourself—begin to have spiritual discernment.

THEN WHAT'S NEXT TO DO?

"For everyone who asks receives."

LUKE 11:10

We will have yearnings and desires for certain things, but not until we are at the limit of desperation will we ask. It is the sense of not being spiritually real that causes us to ask. Have you ever asked out of the depths of your total insufficiency and poverty? Once you realize you are not spiritually real, ask God for the Holy Spirit. The Holy Spirit is the One who makes everything that Jesus did for you real in your life.

AND AFTER THAT WHAT'S NEXT TO DO?

"Seek, and you will find."

LUKE 11:9

If you ask for things from life instead of from God, "you ask amiss"; that is, you ask out of your desire for self-fulfillment. The more you fulfill yourself, the less you will seek God. Get to work—narrow your focus and interests to this one thing. Remember that you can never give another person what you have found, but you can cause him to have a desire for it.

GETTING THERE

"Come to Me."

MATTHEW 11:28

*W*here sin and sorrow stops and the song of the saint starts. Do I really want to get there? I can right now. The questions that truly matter in life are remarkably few, and they are all answered by these words—"Come to Me." If I will simply come to Jesus, my real life will be brought into harmony with my real desires. I will actually cease from sin and will find the song of the Lord beginning in my life.

GETTING THERE

"Where are You staying?"...
"Come and see."..."Follow Me."

JOHN 1:38–39, 43

*W*here our self-interest sleeps and the real interest is awakened. God writes our new name only on those places in our lives where He has erased our pride, self-sufficiency, and self-interest. Some of us have our new names written only in certain spots, like spiritual measles. And in those areas of our lives we look all right. But don't dare look at us when we are not in that mood. A true disciple is one who has his new name written all over him—self-interest, pride, and self-sufficiency have been completely erased.

GETTING THERE

"Follow Me."

MARK 1:17

Where our individual desire dies and sanctified surrender lives. We have the idea that we can dedicate our gifts to God. However, you cannot dedicate what is not yours. There is actually only one thing you can dedicate to God, and that is your right to yourself. If you will give God your right to yourself, He will make a holy experiment out of you—and His experiments always succeed. The one true mark of a saint of God is the inner creativity that flows from being totally surrendered to Jesus Christ.

GET MOVING!

"Abide in Me."

JOHN 15:4

In the matter of determination. Think of the things that take you out of the position of abiding in Christ. *Get moving*—begin to abide *now.* In the initial stages it will be a continual effort to abide, but as you continue, it will become so much a part of your life that you will abide in Him without any conscious effort. Make the determination to abide in Jesus wherever you are now or wherever you may be placed in the future.

GET MOVING!

But also. . .add. . .

2 PETER 1:5

*I*n the matter of drudgery. No one is born either naturally or supernaturally with character; it must be developed. Nor are we born with habits— we have to form godly habits on the basis of the new life God has placed within us. We are not meant to be seen as God's perfect, bright-shining examples, but to be seen as the everyday essence of ordinary life exhibiting the miracle of His grace.

WILL YOU LAY DOWN YOUR LIFE?

"Greater love has no one than this, than to lay down one's life for his friends. . . . I have called you friends."

JOHN 15:13, 15

Jesus does not ask me to die for Him but to lay down my life for Him. It is much easier to die than to lay down your life day in and day out with the sense of the high calling of God. For thirty-three years Jesus laid down His life to do the will of His Father.

If I am a friend of Jesus, I must deliberately and carefully lay down my life for Him.

BEWARE OF CRITICIZING OTHERS

"Judge not, that you be not judged."

MATTHEW 7:1

Criticism serves to make you harsh, vindictive, and cruel, and leaves you with the soothing and flattering idea that you are somehow superior to others. Jesus says that as His disciple you should cultivate a temperament that is never critical. This will not happen quickly but must be developed over a span of time. You must constantly beware of anything that causes you to think of yourself as a superior person.

KEEP RECOGNIZING JESUS

Peter. . .walked on the water to go to Jesus.
But when he saw that the wind was boisterous, he was afraid.

MATTHEW 14:29–30

We step right out with recognition of God in some things; then self-consideration enters our lives and down we go. If you are truly recognizing your Lord, you have no business being concerned about how and where He engineers your circumstances. Let your actual circumstances be what they may, but keep recognizing Jesus, maintaining complete reliance upon Him.

THE SERVICE OF PASSIONATE DEVOTION

"Do you love Me? . . . Tend My sheep."

JOHN 21:16

A person touched by the Spirit of God suddenly says, "Now I see who Jesus is!"—that is the source of devotion.

If I love Jesus Christ personally and passionately, I can serve humanity, even though people may treat me like a "doormat." The secret of a disciple's life is devotion to Jesus Christ, and the characteristics of that life are its seeming insignificance and its meekness.

HAVE YOU COME TO "WHEN" YET?

*And the LORD restored Job's losses
when he prayed for his friends.*

JOB 42:10

I f you are not now receiving the "hundredfold"
which Jesus promised and not getting insight
into God's Word, then start praying for your
friends. The real business of your life is intercessory
prayer. Whatever circumstances God may place you
in, always pray immediately that His atonement
may be recognized and as fully understood in the
lives of others as it has been in yours. Pray for your
friends *now*, and pray for those with whom you
come in contact *now*.

THE MINISTRY OF
THE INNER LIFE

But you are. . .a royal priesthood.

1 PETER 2:9

We must get to the point of being sick to death of ourselves, until there is no longer any surprise at anything God might tell us about ourselves. We cannot reach and understand the depths of our own meagerness. There is only one place where we are right with God, and that is in Christ Jesus. Once we are there, we have to pour out our lives for all we are worth in this ministry of the inner life.

THE UNCHANGING LAW OF JUDGMENT

"For with what judgment you judge,
you will be judged; and with the measure you use,
it will be measured back to you."

MATTHEW 7:2

It is an eternal law of God. Whatever judgment you give will be the very way you are judged. There is a difference between retaliation and retribution. If you have been shrewd in finding out the shortcomings of others, remember that will be exactly how you will be measured. The way you pay is the way life will pay you back. This eternal law works from God's throne down to us.

"ACQUAINTED WITH GRIEF"

A Man of sorrows and acquainted with grief. . .

ISAIAH 53:3

Sin is blatant mutiny against God, and either sin or God must die in my life. The culmination of sin was the crucifixion of Jesus Christ, and what was true in the history of God on earth will also be true in your history and in mine—that is, sin will kill the life of God in us. It is the only explanation why Jesus Christ came to earth, and it is the explanation of the grief and sorrow of life.

RECONCILING YOURSELF TO THE FACT OF SIN

"This is your hour, and the power of darkness."

LUKE 22:53

Not being reconciled to the fact of sin—not recognizing it and refusing to deal with it—produces all the disasters in life. In your human relationships and friendships, have you reconciled yourself to the fact of sin? If not, just around the next corner you will find yourself trapped and you will compromise with it. But if you will reconcile yourself to the fact of sin, you will realize the danger immediately.

RECEIVING YOURSELF IN THE FIRES OF SORROW

"What shall I say? 'Father, save Me from this hour'?
But for this purpose I came to this hour.
Father, glorify Your name."

JOHN 12:27–28

You can always recognize who has been through the fires of sorrow and received himself, and you know that you can go to him in your moment of trouble and find that he has plenty of time for you. But if a person has not been through the fires of sorrow, he is apt to be contemptuous, having no respect or time for you, only turning you away. If you will receive yourself in the fires of sorrow, God will make you nourishment for other people.

DRAWING ON THE GRACE OF GOD—NOW

We. . .plead with you not to receive the grace of God in vain.

2 CORINTHIANS 6:1

Are you failing to rely on the grace of God? It is not a question of praying and asking God to help you—it is taking the grace of God *now*. Pray *now*—draw on the grace of God in your moment of need. Prayer is the most normal and useful thing; it is not simply a reflex action of your devotion to God. We are very slow to learn to draw on God's grace through prayer.

THE OVERSHADOWING OF GOD'S PERSONAL DELIVERANCE

"I am with you to deliver you," says the LORD.

JEREMIAH 1:8

Wherever God sends us, He will guard our lives. Our personal property and possessions are to be a matter of indifference to us, and our hold on these things should be very loose. If this is not the case, we will have panic, heartache, and distress. Having the proper outlook is evidence of the deeply rooted belief in the overshadowing of God's personal deliverance.

HELD BY THE GRIP OF GOD

*That I may lay hold of that for which Christ Jesus
has also laid hold of me. . .*

PHILIPPIANS 3:12

We are not here to work for God because we
have chosen to do so, but because God has
"laid hold of" us. Keep your soul steadfastly related
to God, and remember that you are called not
simply to convey your testimony but also to preach
the gospel. Every Christian must testify to the truth
of God; there must be the agonizing grip of God's
hand on you.

THE STRICTEST DISCIPLINE

"And if your right hand causes you to sin,
cut it off and cast it from you; for it is more profitable
for you that one of your members perish,
than for your whole body to be cast into hell."

MATTHEW 5:30

Your right hand is one of the best things you have, but Jesus says that if it hinders you in following His precepts, then "cut it off." The principle taught here is the strictest discipline or lesson that ever hit humankind.

DO IT NOW!

"Agree with your adversary quickly."

MATTHEW 5:25

Do it quickly—bring yourself to judgment now. In moral and spiritual matters, you must act immediately. God is determined to have His child as pure, clean, and white as driven snow, and as long as there is disobedience, He will allow His Spirit to use whatever process it may take to bring us to obedience. The fact that we insist on proving that we are right is almost always a clear indication that we have some point of disobedience.

THE INEVITABLE PENALTY

"Assuredly, I say to you, you will by no means get out of there till you have paid the last penny."

MATTHEW 5:26

God urged you to come to judgment immediately when He convicted you, but you did not obey. Then the inevitable process began to work, bringing its inevitable penalty. The moment you are willing for God to change your nature, His re-creating forces will begin to work. He will reach to the very limits of the universe to help you take the right road.

The Conditions of Discipleship

"If anyone comes to Me and does not hate. . .
he cannot be My disciple."

LUKE 14:26

Discipleship means personal, passionate devotion to a Person—our Lord Jesus Christ. There is a vast difference between devotion to a person and devotion to principles or to a cause. Our Lord never proclaimed a cause—He proclaimed personal devotion to Himself. To be a disciple is to be a devoted bondservant motivated by love for the Lord Jesus.

THE CONCENTRATION OF PERSONAL SIN

" Woe is me, for I am undone!
Because I am a man of unclean lips."

ISAIAH 6:5

When I come into the very presence of God, I do not realize that I am a sinner in an indefinite sense, but I suddenly realize and the focus of my attention is directed toward the concentration of sin in a particular area of my life. Our conviction is focused on our specific sin, and we realize what we really are. This is always the sign that a person is in the presence of God.

ONE OF GOD'S GREAT "DON'TS"

Do not fret—it only causes harm.

PSALM 37:8

It is one thing to say, "Do not fret," but something very different to have such a nature that you find yourself unable to fret. This "Do not" must work during our days of difficulty and uncertainty, as well as our peaceful days, or it will never work. Resting in the Lord is not dependent on your external circumstances at all, but on your relationship with God Himself.

DON'T PLAN WITHOUT GOD

Commit your way to the LORD, trust also in Him,
and He shall bring it to pass.

PSALM 37:5

God seems to have a delightful way of upsetting the plans we have made when we have not taken Him into account. Suddenly we realize that we have been making our plans without Him—that we have not even considered Him to be a vital, living factor in the planning of our lives. The only thing that will keep us from even the possibility of worrying is to bring God in as the greatest factor in all of our planning.

VISIONS BECOMING REALITY

The parched ground shall become a pool.

ISAIAH 35:7

Every God-given vision will become real if we will only have patience. Just think of the enormous amount of free time God has! He is never in a hurry. God has to take us into the valley and put us through fires and floods to batter us into shape, until we get to the point where He can trust us with the reality of the vision. He is getting us into the shape of the goal He has for us.

ALL EFFORTS OF WORTH AND EXCELLENCE ARE DIFFICULT

"Enter by the narrow gate. . . . Narrow is the gate, and difficult is the way which leads to life."

MATTHEW 7:13–14

Thank God that He does give us difficult things to do! His salvation is a joyous thing, but it is also something that requires bravery, courage, and holiness. It takes a tremendous amount of discipline to live the worthy and excellent life of a disciple of Jesus in the realities of life. And it is always necessary for us to make an effort to live a life of worth and excellence.

WILL TO BE FAITHFUL

"Choose for yourselves this day whom you will serve."

JOSHUA 24:15

A person's will is embodied in the actions of the whole person. I cannot *give up* my will—I must exercise it, putting it into action. I must *will* to obey, and I must *will* to receive God's Spirit. When God gives me a vision of truth, there is never a question of what He will do, but only of what I will do.

Openly declare to Him, "I will be faithful." *Will* to be faithful—and give other people credit for being faithful, too.

WILL YOU EXAMINE YOURSELF?

"You cannot serve the LORD."

JOSHUA 24:19

Do you have even the slightest reliance on anything or anyone other than God? Is there a remnant of reliance left on any natural quality within you? Are you relying on yourself in any manner? Will you examine yourself by asking these probing questions? Is your relationship with God sufficient for you to expect Him to exhibit His wonderful life in you?

THE SPIRITUALLY LAZY SAINT

*"Let us consider one another in order to stir up love
and good works, not forsaking the assembling
of ourselves together."*

HEBREWS 10:24–25

We are all capable of being spiritually lazy saints. We want to stay off the rough roads of life, and our primary objective is to secure a peaceful retreat from the world. To live a distant, withdrawn, and secluded life is diametrically opposed to spirituality as Jesus Christ taught it.

All we want to hear about is a spiritual retirement from the world. Yet Jesus Christ never encourages the idea of retirement—He says, "Go and tell My brethren" (Matthew 28:10).

THE SPIRITUALLY VIGOROUS SAINT

That I may know Him. . .

PHILIPPIANS 3:10

A spiritually vigorous saint never believes that his circumstances simply happen at random, nor does he ever think of his life as being divided into the secular and the sacred. He sees every situation in which he finds himself as the means of obtaining a greater knowledge of Jesus Christ, and he has an attitude of unrestrained abandon and total surrender about him.

The aim of a spiritually vigorous saint is "that I may know Him."

THE SPIRITUALLY
SELF-SEEKING CHURCH

*Till we all come. . .to the measure of the stature
of the fullness of Christ.*

EPHESIANS 4:13

The church ceases to be spiritual when it becomes self-seeking, only interested in the development of its own organization. The reconciliation of the human race according to His plan means realizing Him not only in our lives individually but also in our lives collectively. We are not here to develop a spiritual life of our own or to enjoy a quiet spiritual retreat. We are here to have the full realization of Jesus Christ, for the purpose of building His body.

THE PRICE OF THE VISION

In the year that King Uzziah died, I saw the Lord.

ISAIAH 6:1

My vision of God is dependent upon the condition of my character. My character determines whether or not truth can even be revealed to me. There must be something in my character that conforms to the likeness of God. What I need is God's surgical procedure—His use of external circumstances to bring about internal purification.

Keep paying the price. Let God see that you are willing to live up to the vision.

SUFFERING AFFLICTIONS AND GOING THE SECOND MILE

"But I tell you not to resist an evil person.
But whoever slaps you on your right cheek,
turn the other to him also."

MATTHEW 5:39

Every time I insist on having my own rights, I hurt the Son of God, while in fact I can prevent Jesus from being hurt if I will take the blow myself. A disciple realizes that it is his Lord's honor that is at stake in his life, not his own honor.

MY LIFE'S SPIRITUAL
HONOR AND DUTY

*I am a debtor both to Greeks and to barbarians,
both to wise and to unwise.*

ROMANS 1:14

M y life's spiritual honor and duty is to fulfill my debt to Christ in relation to lost souls. Every tiny bit of my life that has value I owe to the redemption of Jesus Christ. Am I doing anything to enable Him to bring His redemption into evident reality in the lives of others?

Spend your life for the sake of others as the bondservant of Jesus. That is the true meaning of being broken bread and poured-out wine in real life.

THE CONCEPT OF DIVINE CONTROL

"How much more will your Father who is in heaven give good things to those who ask Him!"

MATTHEW 7:11

Jesus urges us to keep our minds filled with the concept of God's control over everything, which means that a disciple must maintain an attitude of perfect trust and an eagerness to ask and to seek.

Fill your mind with the thought that God is there. God is my Father, He loves me, and I will never think of anything that He will forget, so why should I worry?

THE MIRACLE OF BELIEF

My speech and my preaching were not
with persuasive words.

1 CORINTHIANS 2:4

Belief in Jesus is a miracle produced only by the effectiveness of redemption, not by impressive speech, nor by wooing and persuading, but only by the sheer unaided power of God. The creative power of redemption comes through the preaching of the gospel, but never because of the personality of the preacher.

Anything that flatters me in my preaching of the gospel will result in making me a traitor to Jesus, and I prevent the creative power of His redemption from doing its work.

THE MYSTERY OF BELIEVING

And he said, "Who are You, Lord?"

ACTS 9:5

There is nothing miraculous or mysterious about the things we can explain. We control what we are able to explain; consequently it is only natural to seek an explanation for everything. If one rules another by saying, "You must do this," and "You will do that," he breaks the human spirit, making it unfit for God. A person is simply a slave for obeying, unless behind his obedience is the recognition of a holy God.

THE SUBMISSION OF THE BELIEVER

*"You call Me Teacher and Lord,
and you say well, for so I am."*

JOHN 13:13

Our Lord never insists on having authority over us. No, He leaves us perfectly free to choose—so free, in fact, that we can spit in His face or we can put Him to death, as others have done; and yet He will never say a word. But once His life has been created in me through His redemption, I instantly recognize His right to absolute authority over me. It is a complete and effective domination.

DEPENDENT ON GOD'S PRESENCE

Those who wait on the LORD. . . .shall walk and not faint.

ISAIAH 40:31

Having the reality of God's presence is not dependent on our being in a particular circumstance or place but is only dependent on our determination to keep the Lord before us continually. Our problems arise when we refuse to place our trust in the reality of His presence. If our everyday decisions are not according to His will, He will press through them, bringing restraint to our spirit. Then we must be quiet and wait for the direction of His presence.

THE DOORWAY TO THE KINGDOM

"Blessed are the poor in spirit."

MATTHEW 5:3

Blessed are the poor in spirit." This is the first principle in the kingdom of God. The underlying foundation of Jesus Christ's kingdom is poverty, not possessions; not making decisions for Jesus, but having such a sense of absolute futility that we finally admit, "Lord, I cannot even begin to do it." This is the doorway to the kingdom, and yet it takes us so long to believe that we are actually poor! The knowledge of our own poverty is what brings us to the proper place where Jesus Christ accomplishes His work.

SANCTIFICATION

This is the will of God, your sanctification.

1 THESSALONIANS 4:3

The Death Side. In the process of sanctification, the Spirit of God will strip me down until there is nothing left but myself, and that is the place of death. Am I willing to be myself and nothing more?

When I pray, "Lord, show me what sanctification means for me," He will show me. It means being made one with Jesus. Sanctification is not something Jesus puts in me—it is *Himself* in me.

SANCTIFICATION

But of Him you are in Christ Jesus,
who became for us wisdom from God. . .and sanctification.

1 CORINTHIANS 1:30

The Life Side. The mystery of sanctification is that the perfect qualities of Jesus Christ are imparted as a gift to me, not gradually, but instantly once I enter by faith into the realization that He "became for [me]. . .sanctification." Sanctification means nothing less than the holiness of Jesus becoming mine and being exhibited in my life.

Sanctification means the impartation of the holy qualities of Jesus Christ to me—it is drawing from Jesus the very holiness that was exhibited in Him and that He now exhibits in me.

HIS NATURE AND OUR MOTIVES

*"Unless your righteousness exceeds
the righteousness of the scribes and Pharisees,
you will by no means enter the kingdom of heaven."*

MATTHEW 5:20

The characteristic of a disciple is not that he does good things, but that he is good in his motives, having been made good by the supernatural grace of God. Your motives must be so pure that God Almighty can see nothing to rebuke. The purity that God demands is impossible unless I can be remade within, and that is exactly what Jesus has undertaken to do through His redemption.

AM I BLESSED LIKE THIS?

"Blessed are. . ."

MATTHEW 5:3

The teachings of Jesus are all out of proportion when compared to our natural way of looking at things, and they come to us initially with astonishing discomfort. We gradually have to conform our walk and conversation to the precepts of Jesus Christ as the Holy Spirit applies them to our circumstances. The Sermon on the Mount is not a set of rules and regulations—it is a picture of the life we will live when the Holy Spirit is having His unhindered way with us.

THE WAY TO PURITY

"Out of the heart proceed. . ."

MATTHEW 15:19

Initially we trust in our ignorance, calling it innocence, and next we trust our innocence, calling it purity.

Purity is something far too deep for me to arrive at naturally. But when the Holy Spirit comes into me, He brings into the center of my personal life the very Spirit that was exhibited in the life of Jesus Christ, namely, the *Holy* Spirit, which is absolute unblemished purity.

THE WAY TO KNOWLEDGE

*"If anyone wills to do His will,
he shall know concerning the doctrine. . ."*

JOHN 7:17

The golden rule to follow to obtain spiritual understanding is not one of intellectual pursuit but one of obedience. If a person wants scientific knowledge, then intellectual curiosity must be his guide. But if he desires knowledge and insight into the teachings of Jesus Christ, he can only obtain it through obedience.

Even at the risk of being thought of as fanatical, you must obey what God tells you.

GOD'S PURPOSE OR MINE?

Immediately He made His disciples get into the boat and go before Him to the other side.

MARK 6:45

What is my vision of God's purpose for me? Whatever it may be, His purpose is for me to depend on Him and on His power *now*. If I can stay calm, faithful, and unconfused while in the middle of the turmoil of life, the goal of the purpose of God is being accomplished in me. God is not working toward a particular finish—His purpose is the process itself. It is the process, not the outcome, that is glorifying to God.

DO YOU SEE JESUS IN YOUR CLOUDS?

Behold, He is coming with clouds.

REVELATION 1:7

In the Bible, clouds are always associated with God. Clouds are the sorrows, sufferings, or providential circumstances, within or without our personal lives, which actually seem to contradict the sovereignty of God. Yet it is through these very clouds that the Spirit of God is teaching us how to walk by faith. What a revelation it is to know that sorrow, bereavement, and suffering are actually the clouds that come along with God!

THE TEACHING OF
DISILLUSIONMENT

Jesus did not commit Himself to them. . .
for He knew what was in man.

JOHN 2:24–25

Disillusionment means having no more misconceptions, false impressions, and false judgments in life; it means being free from these deceptions. However, though no longer deceived, our experience of disillusionment may actually leave us cynical and overly critical in our judgment of others. But the disillusionment that comes from God brings us to the point where we see people as they really are, yet without any cynicism or any stinging and bitter criticism.

BECOMING ENTIRELY HIS

But let patience have its perfect work,
that you may be perfect and complete, lacking nothing.

JAMES 1:4

Not only must our relationship to God be right, but the outward expression of that relationship must also be right. Ultimately, God will allow nothing to escape; every detail of our lives is under His scrutiny. He never tires of bringing us back to that one point until we learn the lesson, because His purpose is to produce the finished product.

His wonderful work in us makes us know that overall we are right with Him. Whatever it may be, God will point it out with persistence until we become entirely His.

LEARNING ABOUT HIS WAYS

When Jesus finished commanding His twelve disciples. . .
He departed from there to teach and to preach in their cities.

MATTHEW 11:1

Are we playing the part of an amateur providence, trying to play God's role in the lives of others? Are we so noisy in our instruction of other people that God cannot get near them? We must learn to keep our mouths shut and our spirits alert. God wants to instruct us regarding His Son, and He wants to turn our times of prayer into mounts of transfiguration.

THE TEACHING OF ADVERSITY

*"In the world you will have tribulation;
but be of good cheer, I have overcome the world."*

JOHN 16:33

God does not give us overcoming life—He gives us life as we overcome. The strain of life is what builds our strength. If there is no strain, there will be no strength. Are you asking God to give you life, liberty, and joy? He cannot, unless you are willing to accept the strain. And once you face the strain, you will immediately get the strength. Overcome your own timidity and take the first step.

THE COMPELLING PURPOSE
OF GOD

"Behold, we are going up to Jerusalem."
LUKE 18:31

At the beginning of the Christian life, we have our own ideas as to what God's purpose is. We do what we think is right, and yet the compelling purpose of God remains upon us. The work we do is of no account when compared with the compelling purpose of God. It is simply the scaffolding surrounding His work and His plan. God takes us aside all the time. We have not yet understood all there is to know of the compelling purpose of God.

THE BRAVE FRIENDSHIP OF GOD

Then He took the twelve aside.

LUKE 18:31

God's friendship is with people who know their poverty. He can accomplish nothing with the person who thinks that he is of use to God. As Christians we are not here for our own purpose at all—we are here for the purpose of God, and the two are not the same. We do not know what God's compelling purpose is, but whatever happens, we must maintain our relationship with Him.

THE BEWILDERING CALL OF GOD

*"All things that are written by the prophets
concerning the Son of Man will be accomplished. . . ."
But they understood none of these things.*

LUKE 18:31, 34

The call of God can never be understood absolutely or explained externally; it is a call that can only be perceived and understood internally by our true inner nature. His call is simply to be His friend to accomplish His own purposes. Our real test is in truly believing that God knows what He desires. The things that happen do not happen by chance—they happen entirely by the decree of God.

THE CROSS IN PRAYER

"In that day you will ask in My name."
JOHN 16:26

We often think of the Cross of Christ as something we have to get through, yet we get *through* for the purpose of getting *into* it. The Cross represents only one thing for us—complete, entire, absolute identification with the Lord Jesus Christ—and there is nothing in which this identification is more real to us than prayer.

Have you reached such a level of intimacy with God that the only thing that can account for your prayer life is that it has become one with the prayer life of Jesus Christ?

PRAYER IN THE FATHER'S HOUSE

*"Did you not know that I must be about
My Father's business?"*

LUKE 2:49

The only abiding reality is God Himself, and His order comes to me moment by moment. Am I continually in touch with the reality of God, or do I pray only when things have gone wrong— when there is some disturbance in my life? I must learn to identify myself closely with my Lord in ways of holy fellowship and oneness that some of us have not yet even begun to learn. I must learn to live every moment of my life in my Father's house.

PRAYER IN THE FATHER'S HONOR

*"That Holy One who is to be born
will be called the Son of God."*

LUKE 1:35

Is the Son of God praying in me, bringing honor to the Father, or am I dictating my demands to Him? Is He ministering in me as He did in the time of His manhood here on earth? Is God's Son in me going through His passion, suffering so that His own purposes might be fulfilled? The more a person knows of the inner life of God's most mature saints, the more he sees what God's purpose really is.

PRAYER IN THE FATHER'S HEARING

"Father, I thank You that You have heard Me."

JOHN 11:41

When the Son of God prays, He is mindful and consciously aware of only His Father. God always hears the prayers of His Son, and if the Son of God has been formed in me, the Father will always hear my prayers. But I must see to it that the Son of God is exhibited in my human flesh. When I come into contact with the everyday occurrences of life as an ordinary human being, is the prayer of God's eternal Son to His Father being prayed in me?

THE HOLY SUFFERING
OF THE SAINT

*Let those who suffer according to the will of God
commit their souls to Him in doing good.*

1 PETER 4:19

Choosing to suffer means that there must be something wrong with you, but choosing God's will—even if it means you will suffer—is something very different. No normal, healthy saint ever chooses suffering; he simply chooses God's will, just as Jesus did, whether it means suffering or not.

God places His saints where they will bring the most glory to Him, and we are totally incapable of judging where that may be.

THIS EXPERIENCE MUST COME

So he saw him no more.

2 KINGS 2:12

If you remain true, you will get the sign that God is with you. When you come to your wits' end and feel inclined to panic—don't! Stand true to God, and He will bring out His truth in a way that will make your life an expression of worship. Put into practice what you learned. Make a determination to trust in God.

THE THEOLOGY OF
RESTING IN GOD

"Why are you fearful, O you of little faith?"
MATTHEW 8:26

It is when a crisis arises that we instantly reveal upon whom we rely. If we have been learning to worship God and to place our trust in Him, the crisis will reveal that we can go to the point of breaking, yet without breaking our confidence in Him.

A peaceful resting in God, which means a total oneness with Him, will make us not only blameless in His sight, but also a profound joy to Him.

"Do Not Quench the Spirit"

Do not quench the Spirit.

1 Thessalonians 5:19

Suppose God brings you to a crisis and you almost endure it, but not completely. He will engineer the crisis again, but this time some of the intensity will be lost. You will have less discernment and more humiliation at having disobeyed. If you continue to grieve His Spirit, there will come a time when that crisis cannot be repeated, because you have totally quenched Him. But if you will go on through the crisis, your life will become a hymn of praise to God.

THE DISCIPLINE OF THE LORD

"Do not despise the chastening of the LORD,
nor be discouraged when you are rebuked by Him."

HEBREWS 12:5

It is very easy to grieve the Spirit of God; we do it by despising the discipline of the Lord or by becoming discouraged when He rebukes us. If our experience of being set apart from sin and being made holy through the process of sanctification is still very shallow, we tend to mistake the reality of God for something else.

When the Lord disciplines you, let Him have His way with you. Allow Him to put you into a right-standing relationship before God.

THE EVIDENCE OF
THE NEW BIRTH

"You must be born again."

JOHN 3:7

Am I seeking only for the evidence of God's kingdom, or am I actually recognizing His absolute sovereign control? The new birth gives me a new power of vision by which I begin to discern God's control. His sovereignty was there all the time, but with God being true to His nature, I could not see it until I received His very nature myself.

DOES HE KNOW ME?

He calls. . .by name.

JOHN 10:3

It is possible to know all about doctrine and still not know Jesus. A person's soul is in grave danger when the knowledge of doctrine surpasses Jesus, avoiding intimate touch with Him.

Do I have a personal history with Jesus Christ? The one true sign of discipleship is intimate oneness with Him—a knowledge of Jesus that nothing can shake.

ARE YOU DISCOURAGED
OR DEVOTED?

"You still lack one thing.
Sell all that you have. . .and come, follow Me."

LUKE 18:22

Have I ever heard Jesus say something difficult and unyielding to me? Has He said something personally to me to which I have deliberately listened—something I have heard Him say directly to me? Our Lord knows perfectly well that once His word is truly heard, it will bear fruit sooner or later. What is so terrible is that some of us prevent His words from bearing fruit in our present lives. Will we finally make up our minds to be devoted to Him?

HAVE YOU EVER BEEN SPEECHLESS WITH SORROW?

*But when he heard this, he became very sorrowful,
for he was very rich.*

LUKE 18:23

Has God's Word ever come to you, pointing out an area of your life, requiring you to yield it to Him? Maybe He has pointed out certain personal qualities, desires, and interests, or possibly relationships of your heart and mind. If so, then you have often been speechless with sorrow.

Discouragement is disillusioned self-love, and self-love may be love for my devotion to Jesus—not love for Jesus Himself.

SELF-AWARENESS

"Come to Me."

MATTHEW 11:28

Self-awareness is the first thing that will upset the completeness of our life in God, and self-awareness continually produces a sense of struggling and turmoil in our lives. Self-awareness is not sin, and it can be produced by nervous emotions or by suddenly being dropped into a totally new set of circumstances. Yet it is never God's will that we should be anything less than absolutely complete in Him. If we will come to Him, asking Him to produce Christ-awareness in us, He will always do it.

CHRIST-AWARENESS

"I will give you rest."

MATTHEW 11:28

Whenever anything begins to disintegrate your life with Jesus Christ, turn to Him at once, asking Him to reestablish your rest. Ask the Lord to put awareness of Himself in you, and your self-awareness will disappear. Then He will be your all in all. Beware of allowing your self-awareness to continue. Simply ask the Lord to give you Christ-awareness, and He will steady you until your completeness in Him is absolute.

Christ-awareness will take the place of self-awareness.

THE MINISTRY OF THE UNNOTICED

"Blessed are the poor in spirit."

MATTHEW 5:3

Who are the people who have influenced us most? Certainly not the ones who thought they did, but those who did not have even the slightest idea that they were influencing us.

In the Christian life, godly influence is never conscious of itself. If we are conscious of our influence, it ceases to have the genuine loveliness which is characteristic of the touch of Jesus. We always know when Jesus is at work because He produces in the commonplace something that is inspiring.

"I INDEED. . .BUT HE. . ."

*"I indeed baptize you with water. . .but He. . .
will baptize you with the Holy Spirit and fire."*

MATTHEW 3:11

Have I ever come to the point in my life where I can say, "I indeed. . .but He. . ."? *I indeed* am at the end, and I cannot do anything more—*but He* begins right there—He does the things that no one else can ever do.

I indeed was this in the past, *but He* came and something miraculous happened. Get to the end of yourself where you can do nothing, but where He does everything.

PRAYER—BATTLE IN "THE SECRET PLACE"

*"When you pray, go into your room, and. . .
pray to your Father who is in the secret place."*

MATTHEW 6:6

We must have a specially selected place for prayer. Having a secret stillness before God means deliberately shutting the door on our emotions and remembering Him. God is in secret, and He sees us from "the secret place." When we truly live in "the secret place," it becomes impossible for us to doubt God. We become more sure of Him than of anyone or anything else. Enter into "the secret place," and you will find that God was right in the middle of your everyday circumstances all the time.

THE SPIRITUAL SEARCH

"Or what man is there among you who,
if his son asks for bread, will give him a stone?"

MATTHEW 7:9

Never say that it is not God's will to give you what you ask. Don't faint and give up, but find out the reason you have not received; increase the intensity of your search and examine the evidence.

For most of us, prayer simply becomes some trivial religious expression, a matter of mystical and emotional fellowship with God. If we will search out and examine the evidence, we will see very clearly what is wrong. There is no use praying unless we are living as children of God.

SACRIFICE AND FRIENDSHIP

"I have called you friends."

JOHN 15:15

We will never know the joy of self-sacrifice until we surrender in every detail of our lives. Yet self-surrender is the most difficult thing for us to do.

But as soon as we do totally surrender, the Holy Spirit gives us a taste of His joy. The ultimate goal of self-sacrifice is to lay down our lives for our Friend.

Our friendship with Jesus is based on the new life that is completely humble, pure, and devoted to God.

ARE YOU EVER TROUBLED?

"Peace I leave with you, My peace I give to you."
JOHN 14:27

Are you severely troubled right now? Are you afraid and confused by the waves and the turbulence God sovereignly allows to enter your life? Then look up and receive the quiet contentment of the Lord Jesus. Reflecting His peace is proof that you are right with God. Allowing anything to hide the face of Jesus Christ from you either causes you to become troubled or gives you a false sense of security.

LIVING YOUR THEOLOGY

"Walk while you have the light, lest darkness overtake you."
JOHN 12:35

Your theology must work itself out, exhibiting itself in your most common everyday relationships. You may know all about the doctrine of sanctification, but are you working it out in the everyday issues of your life? Every detail of your life, whether physical, moral, or spiritual, is to be judged and measured by the standard of the atonement by the Cross of Christ.

THE PURPOSE OF PRAYER

"Lord, teach us to pray."

LUKE 11:1

To say that "prayer changes things" is not as close to the truth as saying, "Prayer changes *me*, and then I change things." God has established things so that prayer, on the basis of redemption, changes the way a person looks at things. Prayer is not a matter of changing things externally, but one of working miracles in a person's inner nature.

THE UNSURPASSED INTIMACY OF TESTED FAITH

"Did I not say to you that if you would believe you would see the glory of God?"

JOHN 11:40

Faith must be tested, because it can only become your intimate possession through conflict. What is challenging your faith right now? The test will either prove your faith right, or it will kill it. There is continual testing in the life of faith up to the point of our physical death, which is the last great test. Faith is absolute trust in God—trust that could never imagine that He would forsake us.

USEFULNESS OR RELATIONSHIP?

"Nevertheless do not rejoice in this. . .
but rather rejoice because your names
are written in heaven."

LUKE 10:20

Our tendency today is to put the emphasis on service. If you make usefulness the test, then Jesus Christ was the greatest failure who ever lived. For the saint, direction and guidance come from God Himself, not some measure of that saint's usefulness. It is the work that God does through us that counts, not what we do for Him. All that our Lord gives His attention to in a person's life is that person's relationship with God—something of great value to His Father.

"MY JOY...YOUR JOY"

*"That My joy may remain in you,
and that your joy may be full..."*

JOHN 15:11

What was the joy that Jesus had? Joy should not be confused with happiness. In fact, it is an insult to Jesus Christ to use the word *happiness* in connection with Him. The joy of Jesus was His absolute self-surrender and self-sacrifice to His Father—the joy of doing that which the Father sent Him to do. Jesus prayed that our joy might continue fulfilling itself until it becomes the same joy as His. Have I allowed Jesus Christ to introduce His joy to me?

DESTINED TO BE HOLY

"Be holy, for I am holy."

1 PETER 1:16

Never tolerate, because of sympathy for yourself or for others, any practice that is not in keeping with a holy God. Holiness means absolute purity of your walk before God, the words coming from your mouth, and every thought in your mind—placing every detail of your life under the scrutiny of God Himself. Holiness is not simply what God gives me, but what God has given me that is being exhibited in my life.

A LIFE OF PURE
AND HOLY SACRIFICE

"He who believes in Me. . .out of his heart will flow. . ."

JOHN 7:38

When Mary broke the "flask of very costly oil. . .and poured it on [Jesus'] head," it was an act for which no one else saw any special occasion (Mark 14:3–4). But Jesus commended Mary for her extravagant act of devotion. Our Lord is filled with overflowing joy whenever He sees any of us doing what Mary did—not being bound by a particular set of rules, but being totally surrendered to Him.

POURING OUT THE WATER
OF SATISFACTION

Nevertheless he would not drink it,
but poured it out to the LORD.

2 SAMUEL 23:16

You can never set apart for God something that you desire for yourself to achieve your own satisfaction. If you try to satisfy yourself with a blessing from God, it will corrupt you. You must sacrifice it, pouring it out to God—something that your common sense says is an absurd waste.

If you have become bitter and sour, it is because when God gave you a blessing you hoarded it. Yet if you had poured it out to Him, you would have been the sweetest person on earth.

His!

"They were Yours, You gave them to Me."

JOHN 17:6

O ur Lord makes His disciple His very own possession, becoming responsible for him. The desire that comes into a disciple is not one of *doing* anything for Jesus, but of *being* a perfect delight to Him. The secret is truly being able to say, "I am His, and He is accomplishing His work and His purposes through me."

Be entirely His!

WATCHING WITH JESUS

"Watch with Me."

MATTHEW 26:40

In the early stages of our Christian life, we do not watch *with* Jesus; we watch *for* Him. Our Lord is trying to introduce us to identification with Himself through a particular "Gethsemane" experience of our own. But we refuse to go, saying, "No, Lord, I can't see the meaning of this, and besides, it's very painful." We don't know how to watch with Him—we are only used to the idea of Jesus watching with us. Watch *with* Him.

THE FAR-REACHING RIVERS OF LIFE

"Rivers of living water. . ."
JOHN 7:38

The river of the Spirit of God overcomes all obstacles. Never focus your eyes on the obstacle or the difficulty. The obstacle will be a matter of total indifference to the river that will flow steadily through you if you will simply remember to stay focused on the Source. Never allow anything to come between you and Jesus Christ—not emotion nor experience—nothing must keep you from the one great sovereign Source.

FOUNTAINS OF BLESSINGS

"The water that I shall give him will become in him a fountain of water."

JOHN 4:14

We are to be fountains through which Jesus can flow as "rivers of living water" in blessing to everyone. As surely as we receive blessings from Him, He will pour out blessings through us. It is not a blessing that you pass on, or an experience that you share with others, but a river that continually flows through you. Stay at the Source, closely guarding your faith in Jesus Christ and your relationship to Him, and there will be a steady flow into the lives of others.

DO IT YOURSELF

*"Casting down arguments and every high thing that
exalts itself against the knowledge of God. . ."*

2 CORINTHIANS 10:5

*D*eterminedly Demolish Some Things. God does
not make us holy in the sense that He makes
our character holy. He makes us holy in the sense
that He has made us innocent before Him. And
then we have to turn that innocence into holy
character through the moral choices we make.
These choices are continually opposed and hostile
to the things of our natural life which have become
so deeply entrenched. We can either turn back,
making ourselves of no value to the kingdom of
God, or we can determinedly demolish these things.

DO IT YOURSELF

*Bringing every thought into captivity
to the obedience of Christ. . .*

2 CORINTHIANS 10:5

*D*eterminedly Discipline Other Things. True
determination and zeal are found in obeying
God, not in the inclination to serve Him. It is
inconceivable, but true nevertheless, that saints are
simply doing work for God that has been instigated
by their own human nature and has not been made
spiritual through determined discipline.

We have a tendency to forget that a person is
not only committed to Jesus Christ for salvation
but also committed, responsible, and accountable to
Jesus Christ's view of God, the world, and sin.

MISSIONARY WEAPONS

"When you were under the fig tree, I saw you."
JOHN 1:48

Worshipping in Everyday Occasions. A private relationship of worshipping God is the greatest essential element of spiritual fitness. If your worship is right in your private relationship with God, then when He sets you free, you will be ready. It is in the unseen life, which only God has seen, that you have become perfectly fit. And when the strain of the crisis comes, you can be relied upon by God.

God's training ground, where the missionary weapons are found, is the hidden, personal, worshipping life of the saint.

MISSIONARY WEAPONS

*"If I then, your Lord and Teacher, have washed your feet,
you also ought to wash one another's feet."*

JOHN 13:14

Ministering in Everyday Opportunities. The things Jesus did were the most menial of everyday tasks, and this is an indication that it takes all of God's power in me to accomplish even the most common tasks in His way. Can I use a towel as He did? Towels, dishes, sandals, and all the other ordinary things in our lives reveal what we are made of more quickly than anything else. It takes God Almighty incarnate in us to do the most menial duty as it ought to be done.

GOING THROUGH SPIRITUAL CONFUSION

"You do not know what you ask."

MATTHEW 20:22

There are times in your spiritual life when there is confusion, and the way out of it is not simply to say that you should not be confused. It is not a matter of right and wrong, but a matter of God taking you through a way that you temporarily do not understand. And it is only by going through the spiritual confusion that you will come to the understanding of what God wants for you.

AFTER SURRENDER—
THEN WHAT?

"I have finished the work which You have given Me to do."

JOHN 17:4

True surrender is not simply surrender of our external life but surrender of our will—and once that is done, surrender is complete. The greatest crisis we ever face is the surrender of our will. Yet God never forces a person's will into surrender, and He never begs. He patiently waits until that person willingly yields to Him. And once that battle has been fought, it never needs to be fought again.

ARGUMENTS OR OBEDIENCE?

"The simplicity that is in Christ. . ."

2 CORINTHIANS 11:3

You cannot think through spiritual confusion to make things clear; to make things clear, you must obey. In intellectual matters you can think things out, but in spiritual matters you will only think yourself into further wandering thoughts and more confusion. If there is something in your life upon which God has put His pressure, then obey Him in that matter. Bring all your "arguments and. . .every thought into captivity to the obedience of Christ" regarding the matter, and everything will become as clear as daylight to you (2 Corinthians 10:5).

WHAT TO RENOUNCE

But we have renounced the hidden things of shame.

2 CORINTHIANS 4:2

Have you "renounced the hidden things of shame" in your life—the things that your sense of honor or pride will not allow to come into the light? Renounce everything in its entirety until there is no hidden dishonesty or craftiness about you at all. You must maintain continual watchfulness so that nothing arises in your life that would cause you shame.

PRAYING TO GOD IN SECRET

"But you, when you pray, go into your room,
and when you have shut your door,
pray to your Father who is in the secret place."

MATTHEW 6:6

Keep your eyes on God, not on people. Your motivation should not be the desire to be known as a praying person. Find an inner room in which to pray where no one even knows you are praying, shut the door, and talk to God in secret. Have no motivation other than to know your Father in heaven. It is impossible to carry on your life as a disciple without definite times of secret prayer.

IS THERE GOOD IN TEMPTATION?

No temptation has overtaken you
except such as is common to man.

1 CORINTHIANS 10:13

Temptation is not something we can escape; in fact, it is essential to the well-rounded life of a person. Beware of thinking that you are tempted as no one else—what you go through is the common inheritance of the human race, not something that no one has ever before endured. God does not save us from temptations—He sustains us in the midst of them.

HIS TEMPTATION AND OURS

For we do not have a High Priest
who cannot sympathize with our weaknesses,
but was in all points tempted as we are, yet without sin.

HEBREWS 4:15

Our Lord's temptations and ours are in different realms until we are born again and become His brothers. The temptations of Jesus are not those of a mere man, but the temptations of God as Man. Through regeneration, the Son of God is formed in us, and in our physical life He has the same setting that He had on earth. Only the Spirit of God can detect temptation of the devil.

ARE YOU GOING ON WITH JESUS?

"But you are those who have continued with Me in My trials."

LUKE 22:28

It is true that Jesus Christ is with us through our temptations, but are we going on with Him through His temptations? Many of us turn back from going on with Jesus from the very moment we have an experience of what He can do. Watch when God changes your circumstances to see whether you are going on with Jesus or siding with the world, the flesh, and the devil. We wear His name, but are we going on with Him?

THE DIVINE COMMANDMENT
OF LIFE

*"Therefore you shall be perfect,
just as your Father in heaven is perfect."*

MATTHEW 5:48

Our Lord's exhortation to us is to be generous in our behavior toward everyone. Beware of living according to your natural affections in your spiritual life. Everyone has natural affections—some people we like and others we don't like. Yet we must never let those likes and dislikes rule our Christian life.

The true expression of Christian character is not in good-doing but in Godlikeness.

THE MISSIONARY'S PREDESTINED PURPOSE

*"And now the LORD says, who formed Me
from the womb to be His Servant. . ."*

ISAIAH 49:5

We must continually keep our soul open to the fact of God's creative purpose and never confuse or cloud it with our own intentions. If we do, God will have to force our intentions aside no matter how much it may hurt. A missionary is created for the purpose of being God's servant, one in whom God is glorified.

Beware lest you forget God's purpose for your life.

THE MISSIONARY'S MASTER AND TEACHER

"You call Me Teacher and Lord,
and you say well, for so I am."

JOHN 13:13

If we are consciously aware that we are being mastered, that idea itself is proof that we have no master. If that is our attitude toward Jesus, we are far away from having the relationship He wants with us. He wants us in a relationship where He is so easily our Master and Teacher that we have no conscious awareness of it—a relationship where all we know is that we are His to obey.

THE MISSIONARY'S GOAL

"Behold, we are going up to Jerusalem."

LUKE 18:31

In the Christian life the goal is given at the very beginning, and the beginning and the end are exactly the same, namely, our Lord Himself. We start with Christ and we end with Him, not simply to our own idea of what the Christian life should be. The goal of the missionary is to do God's will, not to be useful or to win the lost. A missionary *is* useful and he *does* win the lost, but his goal is to do the will of his Lord.

The "Go" of Preparation

*"Therefore if you bring your gift to the altar,
and there remember that your brother has something against
you, leave your gift there before the altar,
and go your way. First be reconciled to your brother,
and then come and offer your gift."*

MATTHEW 5:23–24

The "go" of preparation is to allow the Word of God to examine you closely. Do you have anything to hide from God? If you do, then let God search you with His light. If there is sin in your life, don't just *admit* it—*confess* it. Are you willing to obey your Lord and Master?

THE "GO" OF RELATIONSHIP

"And whoever compels you to go one mile, go with him two."
MATTHEW 5:41

No amount of enthusiasm will ever stand up to the strain that Jesus Christ will put upon His servant. Only one thing will bear the strain, and that is a personal relationship with Jesus Christ Himself—a relationship that has been examined, purified, and tested until only one purpose remains and I can truly say, "I am here for God to send me where He will." Everything else may become blurred, but this relationship with Jesus Christ must never be.

THE "GO" OF RECONCILIATION

"If you. . .remember that your brother
has something against you. . ."

MATTHEW 5:23

The process of reconciliation is clearly marked. First we have the heroic spirit of self-sacrifice, then the sudden restraint by the sensitivity of the Holy Spirit, and then we are stopped at the point of our conviction. This is followed by obedience to the Word of God, which builds an attitude that places no blame on the one with whom you have been in the wrong. And finally there is the glad, simple, unhindered offering of your gift to God.

THE "GO" OF RENUNCIATION

"Lord, I will follow You wherever You go."

LUKE 9:57

Never apologize for your Lord. The words of the Lord hurt and offend until there is nothing left to be hurt or offended. Jesus Christ had no tenderness whatsoever toward anything that was ultimately going to ruin a person in his service to God. If the Spirit of God brings to your mind a word of the Lord that hurts you, you can be sure that there is something in you that He wants to hurt to the point of its death.

THE "GO" OF UNCONDITIONAL IDENTIFICATION

"One thing you lack. . .come, take up the cross, and follow Me."

MARK 10:21

Jesus' primary consideration is my absolute annihilation of my right to myself and my identification with Him, which means having a relationship with Him in which there are no other relationships. Very few of us truly know what is meant by the absolute "go" of unconditional identification with, and abandonment and surrender to, Jesus.

I must humble myself until I am merely a living person.

THE AWARENESS OF THE CALL

For necessity is laid upon me; yes,
woe is me if I do not preach the gospel!

1 CORINTHIANS 9:16

If a man or woman is called of God, it doesn't matter how difficult the circumstances may be. God orchestrates every force at work for His purpose in the end. If you will agree with God's purpose, He will bring not only your conscious level but also all the deeper levels of your life, which you yourself cannot reach, into perfect harmony.

THE ASSIGNING OF THE CALL

*I now rejoice in my sufferings for you, and fill up in my
flesh what is lacking in the afflictions of Christ,
for the sake of His body.*

COLOSSIANS 1:24

To be a holy person means that the elements of our natural life experience the very presence of God as they are providentially broken in His service. We have to be placed into God and brought into agreement with Him before we can be broken bread in His hands. Stay right with God and let Him do as He likes, and you will find that He is producing the kind of bread and wine that will benefit His other children.

THE PLACE OF EXALTATION

Jesus. . .led them up on a high mountain apart by themselves.

MARK 9:2

We have all experienced times of exaltation on the mountain, when we have seen things from God's perspective and have wanted to stay there. But God will never allow us to stay there. The true test of our spiritual life is in exhibiting the power to descend from the mountain. It is a wonderful thing to be on the mountain with God, but a person only gets there so that he may later go down and lift up the people in the valley.

THE PLACE OF HUMILIATION

"If You can do anything, have compassion on us and help us."
MARK 9:22

I t is in the place of humiliation that we find
our true worth to God—that is where our
faithfulness is revealed. Most of us can do things if
we are always at some heroic level of intensity, simply
because of the natural selfishness of our own hearts.
But God wants us to be at the drab everyday level,
where we live in the valley according to our personal
relationship with Him.

THE PLACE OF MINISTRY

"This kind can come out by nothing but prayer and fasting."
MARK 9:29

Your duty in service and ministry is to see that there is nothing between Jesus and yourself. Is there anything between you and Jesus even now? If there is, you must get through it, not by ignoring it as an irritation, or by going up and over it, but by facing it and getting through it into the presence of Jesus Christ. Then that very problem will glorify Jesus Christ in a way that you will never know until you see Him face-to-face.

THE VISION AND THE REALITY

Called to be saints. . .

1 CORINTHIANS 1:2

Thank God for being able to see all that you have not yet been. You have had the vision, but you are not yet to the reality of it by any means. We are not quite prepared for the bumps and bruises that must come if we are going to be turned into the shape of the vision. We have seen what we are not, and what God wants us to be, but are we willing to be battered into the shape of the vision to be used by God?

THE NATURE OF DEGENERATION

*Therefore, just as through one man sin entered the world,
and death through sin, and thus death spread to all men,
because all sinned.*

ROMANS 5:12

The nature of sin is not immorality and wrongdoing, but the nature of self-realization which leads us to say, "I am my own god." This nature may exhibit itself in proper morality or in improper immorality, but it always has a common basis—my claim to my right to myself. When our Lord faced people, He paid no attention to the moral degradation of one nor any attention to the moral attainment of the other. He looked at something we do not see, namely, the nature of man.

THE NATURE OF REGENERATION

When it pleased God. . .to reveal His Son in me. . .
GALATIANS 1:15-16

If Jesus Christ is truly a regenerator, someone who can put His own heredity of holiness into me, then I can begin to see what He means when He says that I have to be holy. Redemption means that Jesus Christ can put into anyone the hereditary nature that was in Himself. The proper action on my part is simply to agree with God's verdict on sin as judged on the Cross of Christ.

THE NATURE OF RECONCILIATION

For He made Him who knew no sin to be sin for us,
that we might become the righteousness of God in Him.

2 CORINTHIANS 5:21

Our Lord took on Himself the sin of the world through *identification with us*, not through *sympathy* for us. He deliberately took on His own shoulders, and endured in His own body, the complete, cumulative sin of the human race. Jesus Christ reconciled the human race, putting it back to where God designed it to be. And now anyone can experience that reconciliation, being brought into oneness with God.

COMING TO JESUS

"Come to Me."

MATTHEW 11:28

How often have you come to God with your requests and gone away thinking, "I've really received what I wanted this time!" And yet you go away with nothing, while all the time God has stood with His hands outstretched not only to take you but also for you to take Him. Just think of the invincible, unconquerable, and untiring patience of Jesus, who lovingly says, "Come to Me. . . ."

BUILDING ON THE ATONEMENT

Present your members as slaves of righteousness for holiness.
ROMANS 6:19

The atonement of Jesus must be exhibited in practical, unassuming ways in my life. Every time I obey, the absolute deity of God is on my side, so that the grace of God and my natural obedience are in perfect agreement. Obedience means that I have completely placed my trust in the atonement, and my obedience is immediately met by the delight of the supernatural grace of God.

HOW WILL I KNOW?

"I thank You, Father. . .that You have hidden these things from the wise and prudent and have revealed them to babes."

MATTHEW 11:25

The only way you can get to know the truth of God is to stop trying to find out and by being born again. If you obey God in the first thing He shows you, then He instantly opens up the next truth to you. God will never reveal more truth about Himself to you until you have obeyed what you know already.

GOD'S SILENCE—THEN WHAT?

When He heard that he was sick,
He stayed two more days in the place where He was.

JOHN 11:6

A wonderful thing about God's silence is that His stillness is contagious—it gets into you, causing you to become perfectly confident so that you can honestly say, "I know that God has heard me." His silence is the very proof that He has. If Jesus Christ is bringing you into the understanding that prayer is for the glorifying of His Father, then He will give you the first sign of His intimacy—silence.

GETTING INTO GOD'S STRIDE

Enoch walked with God.

GENESIS 5:24

It is painful work to get in step with God and to keep pace with Him—it means getting your second wind spiritually. In learning to walk with God, there is always the difficulty of getting into His stride, but once we have done so, the only characteristic that exhibits itself is the very life of God Himself. The individual person is merged into a personal oneness with God, and God's stride and His power alone are exhibited.

INDIVIDUAL DISCOURAGEMENT AND PERSONAL GROWTH

Moses. . .went out to his brethren and looked at their burdens.

EXODUS 2:11

We may have the vision of God and a very clear understanding of what God wants, and yet when we start to do it, there comes to us something equivalent to Moses' forty years in the wilderness. It's as if God had ignored the entire thing, and when we are thoroughly discouraged, God comes back and revives His call to us. If you are going through a time of discouragement, there is a time of great personal growth ahead.

THE KEY TO THE MISSIONARY'S WORK

*"All authority has been given to Me in heaven and on earth.
Go therefore and make disciples of all the nations."*

MATTHEW 28:18–19

The key to the missionary's work is the authority of Jesus Christ, not the needs of the lost. We are inclined to look on our Lord as one who assists us in our endeavors for God. Yet our Lord places Himself as the absolute sovereign and supreme Lord over His disciples. He does not say that the lost will never be saved if we don't go—He simply says, "Go therefore and make disciples of all the nations."

THE KEY TO THE MISSIONARY'S MESSAGE

*And He Himself is the propitiation for our sins,
and not for ours only but also for the whole world.*

1 JOHN 2:2

The key to the missionary's message is the propitiation of Christ Jesus—His sacrifice for us that completely satisfied the wrath of God. Look at any other aspect of Christ's work, whether it is healing, saving, or sanctifying, and you will see that there is nothing limitless about those. The missionary's message is the limitless importance of Jesus Christ as the propitiation for our sins.

THE KEY TO THE MASTER'S ORDERS

"Therefore pray the Lord of the harvest to send out laborers into His harvest."

MATTHEW 9:38

The key to the missionary's difficult task is in the hand of God, and that key is prayer, not work—that is, not work as the word is commonly used today, which often results in the shifting of our focus away from God. The key to the missionary's difficult task is also not the key of common sense, nor is it the key of medicine, civilization, education, or even evangelization. The key is in following the Master's orders—the key is prayer.

THE KEY OF THE GREATER WORK

*"And greater works than these he will do,
because I go to My Father."*

JOHN 14:12

Prayer does not equip us for greater works— prayer is the greater work. Yet we think of prayer as some commonsense exercise of our higher powers that simply prepares us for God's work. The way fruit remains firm is through prayer, but remember that it is prayer based on the agony of Christ in redemption, not on my own agony. We must go to God as His child, because only a child gets his prayers answered.

THE KEY TO THE MISSIONARY'S DEVOTION

They went forth for His name's sake.

3 JOHN 7

The key to the missionary's devotion is that he is attached to nothing and to no one except our Lord Himself. It does not mean simply being detached from the external things surrounding us. Our Lord was amazingly in touch with the ordinary things of life, but He had an inner detachment except toward God. External detachment is often an actual indication of a secret, growing, inner attachment to the things we stay away from externally.

THE UNHEEDED SECRET

"My kingdom is not of this world."

JOHN 18:36

The great enemy of the Lord Jesus Christ today is the idea of practical work that has no basis in the New Testament but comes from the systems of the world. This work insists upon endless energy and activities, but no private life with God. The emphasis is put on the wrong thing. It is a hidden, obscure thing. An active Christian worker too often lives to be seen by others, while it is the innermost, personal area that reveals the power of a person's life.

IS GOD'S WILL MY WILL?

For this is the will of God, your sanctification.

1 THESSALONIANS 4:3

Sanctification is not a question of whether God is willing to sanctify me—is it *my* will? Am I willing to let God do in me everything that has been made possible through the atonement of the Cross of Christ? Recognize your need, but stop longing and make it a matter of action. Receive Jesus Christ to become sanctification for you by absolute, unquestioning faith, and the great miracle of the atonement of Jesus will become real in you.

IMPULSIVENESS OR DISCIPLESHIP?

Building yourselves up on your most holy faith. . .

JUDE 1:20

Impulsiveness is a trait of the natural life, and our Lord always ignores it, because it hinders the development of the life of a disciple. Impulsiveness needs to be trained into intuition through discipline.

Discipleship is built entirely on the supernatural grace of God. It is ingrained in us that we have to do exceptional things for God—but we do not. We have to be exceptional in the ordinary things of life, and holy on the ordinary streets, among ordinary people.

THE WITNESS OF THE SPIRIT

The Spirit Himself bears witness with our spirit.

ROMANS 8:16

The Spirit of God witnesses to the redemption of our Lord and to nothing else. The Spirit witnesses only to His own nature and to the work of redemption, never to our reason. If we are trying to make Him witness to our reason, it is no wonder that we are in darkness and uncertainty. Throw it all overboard, trust in Him, and He will give you the witness of the Spirit.

NOTHING OF THE OLD LIFE!

Therefore, if anyone is in Christ, he is a new creation;
old things have passed away.

2 CORINTHIANS 5:17

How are we going to get a life that has no lust, no self-interest, and is not sensitive to the ridicule of others? The only way is by allowing nothing of the old life to remain and by having only simple, perfect trust in God—such a trust that we no longer want God's blessings but only want God Himself.

THE PROPER PERSPECTIVE

*Now thanks be to God who always leads us
in triumph in Christ.*

2 CORINTHIANS 2:14

The proper perspective of a servant of God must not simply be as near to the highest as he can get, but it must be *the* highest. Be careful that you vigorously maintain God's perspective, and remember that it must be done every day, little by little. Don't think on a finite level. No outside power can touch the proper perspective.

SUBMITTING TO GOD'S PURPOSE

I have become all things to all men,
that I might by all means save some.

1 CORINTHIANS 9:22

All of God's people are ordinary people who have been made extraordinary by the purpose He has given them. Unless we have the right purpose intellectually in our minds and lovingly in our hearts, we will very quickly be diverted from being useful to God. We are not workers for God by choice. Many people deliberately choose to be workers, but they have no purpose of God's almighty grace or His mighty Word in them.

Let Him have His way.

WHAT IS A MISSIONARY?

"As the Father has sent Me, I also send you."

JOHN 20:21

A missionary is someone sent by Jesus Christ just as He was sent by God. The great controlling factor is not the needs of people but the command of Jesus. The source of our inspiration in our service for God is behind us. The tendency today is to put the inspiration out in front—to sweep everything together in front of us and make it conform to our definition of success. But in the New Testament the inspiration is put behind us and is the Lord Jesus Himself. The goal is to carry out *His* plans.

THE METHOD OF MISSIONS

"Go therefore and make disciples of all the nations."
MATTHEW 28:19

The one great challenge to us is—do I know my risen Lord? Do I know the power of His indwelling Spirit? Am I wise enough in God's sight, but foolish enough according to the wisdom of the world, to trust in what Jesus Christ has said? Or am I abandoning the great supernatural position of limitless confidence in Christ Jesus, which is really God's only call for a missionary? If I follow any other method, I depart altogether from the methods prescribed by our Lord.

JUSTIFICATION BY FAITH

For if when we were enemies we were reconciled to God
through the death of His Son, much more,
having been reconciled, we shall be saved by His life.

ROMANS 5:10

When I turn to God and by belief accept what God reveals, the miraculous atonement by the Cross of Christ instantly places me into a right relationship with God. And as a result of the supernatural miracle of God's grace, I stand justified, not because I am sorry for my sin, or because I have repented, but because of what Jesus has done.

SUBSTITUTION

*He made Him. . .to be sin for us, that we might become
the righteousness of God in Him.*

2 CORINTHIANS 5:21

Our sins are removed because of the death
of Jesus, and the only explanation for His
death is His obedience to His Father, not His
sympathy for us. We are acceptable to God not
because we have obeyed, nor because we have
promised to give up things, but because of the
death of Christ, and for no other reason. Through
identification with His death I can be freed from
sin and have His very righteousness imparted as a
gift to me.

FAITH

Without faith it is impossible to please Him.

HEBREWS 11:6

Faith always works in a personal way, because the purpose of God is to see that perfect faith is made real in His children. Faith is a tremendously active principle that always puts Jesus Christ first. Our faith is limitless. Faith is the entire person in the right relationship with God through the power of the Spirit of Jesus Christ.

THE TRIAL OF FAITH

"Faith as a mustard seed. . ."

MATTHEW 17:20

Faith by its very nature must be tested and tried. And the real trial of faith is not that we find it difficult to trust God, but that God's character must be proven as trustworthy in our own minds. Faith being worked out into reality must experience times of unbroken isolation. Never confuse the trial of faith with the ordinary discipline of life, because a great deal of what we call the trial of faith is the inevitable result of being alive.

"YOU ARE NOT YOUR OWN"

Do you not know. . .you are not your own?

1 CORINTHIANS 6:19

We are called into intimacy with the gospel, and things happen that appear to have nothing to do with us. But God is getting us into fellowship with Himself. Let Him have His way. If you refuse, you will be of no value to God in His redemptive work in the world, but will be a hindrance and a stumbling block.

OBEDIENCE OR INDEPENDENCE?

"If you love Me, keep My commandments."

JOHN 14:15

The Lord does not give me rules, but He makes His standard very clear. If my relationship to Him is that of love, I will do what He says without hesitation. If I hesitate, it is because I love someone I have placed in competition with Him, namely, myself. Jesus Christ will not force me to obey Him, but I must. If I obey Jesus Christ in the seemingly random circumstances of life, they become pinholes through which I see the face of God.

A BONDSERVANT OF JESUS

I have been crucified with Christ;
it is no longer I who live, but Christ lives in me.

GALATIANS 2:20

Has that breaking of my independence come? Will I surrender to Jesus Christ, placing no conditions whatsoever as to how the brokenness will come? I must be broken from my own understanding of myself. When I reach that point, immediately the reality of the supernatural identification with Jesus Christ takes place.

The passion of Christianity comes from deliberately signing away my own rights and becoming a bondservant of Jesus Christ. Until I do that, I will not begin to be a saint.

THE AUTHORITY OF TRUTH

Draw near to God and He will draw near to you.

JAMES 4:8

It is essential that you give people the opportunity to act on the truth of God. The responsibility must be left with the individual—you cannot act for him. It must be his own deliberate act, but the evangelical message should always lead him to action. Refusing to act leaves a person paralyzed, exactly where he was previously. But once he acts, he is never the same. The moments I truly live are the moments when I act with my entire will.

PARTAKERS OF HIS SUFFERINGS

Rejoice to the extent that you partake of Christ's sufferings.

I PETER 4:13

If you are going to be used by God, He will take you through a number of experiences that are not meant for you personally at all. They are designed to make you useful in His hands and to enable you to understand what takes place in the lives of others. Because of this process, you will never be surprised by what comes your way.

INTIMATE THEOLOGY

"Do you believe this?"

JOHN 11:26

Is Jesus teaching you to have a personal intimacy with Himself? Allow Him to drive His question home to you—"Do you believe *this?*" Are you facing an area of doubt in your life? Have you come to a crossroads of overwhelming circumstances where your theology is about to become a very personal belief? This happens only when a personal problem brings the awareness of our personal need.

THE UNDETECTED SACREDNESS OF CIRCUMSTANCES

All things work together for good to those who love God.
ROMANS 8:28

The circumstances of a saint's life are ordained of God. In the life of a saint there is no such thing as chance. God by His providence brings you into circumstances that you can't understand at all, but the Spirit of God understands. God brings you to places, among people, and into certain conditions to accomplish a definite purpose. All your circumstances are in the hand of God.

THE UNRIVALED POWER OF PRAYER

We do not know what we should pray for as we ought,
but the Spirit Himself makes intercession for us
with groanings which cannot be uttered.

ROMANS 8:26

We know what it is to pray in accordance with the Spirit, but we don't often realize that the Holy Spirit Himself prays prayers in us which we cannot utter ourselves. He expresses for us the unutterable.

God searches your heart, not to know what your conscious prayers are, but to find out what the prayer of the Holy Spirit is.

SACRED SERVICE

I now rejoice in my sufferings for you, and fill up in my flesh what is lacking in the afflictions of Christ.

COLOSSIANS 1:24

The Christian worker must be so closely identified with his Lord and the reality of His redemption that Christ can continually bring His creating life through him. When we preach the historical facts of the life and death of our Lord as they are conveyed in the New Testament, our words are made sacred. God uses these words, on the basis of His redemption, to create something in those who listen which otherwise could never have been created.

FELLOWSHIP IN THE GOSPEL

Fellow laborer in the gospel of Christ. . .

1 THESSALONIANS 3:2

I must learn that the purpose of my life belongs to God, not me. God is using me from His great personal perspective, and all He asks of me is that I trust Him. When I stop telling God what I want, He can freely work His will in me without any hindrance. He can crush me, exalt me, or do anything else He chooses. He simply asks me to have absolute faith in Him and His goodness.

The Supreme Climb

"Take now your son. . ."

Genesis 22:2

God's command is "Take *now*," not later. We know something is right, but we try to find excuses for not doing it immediately. If we are to climb to the height God reveals, it can never be done later—it must be done now. And the sacrifice must be worked through our will before we actually perform it.

If the providential will of God means a hard and difficult time for you, go through it. By going through the trial you learn to know God better.

THE CHANGED LIFE

If anyone is in Christ, he is a new creation;
old things have passed away;
behold, all things have become new.

2 CORINTHIANS 5:17

The work of salvation means that in your life things are dramatically changed. You no longer look at things in the same way. Your desires are new and the old things have lost their power to attract you. Has God changed the things that really matter to you? If you are born again, the Spirit of God makes the change very evident in your life and thought. It is this complete and amazing change that is the very evidence that you are saved.

FAITH OR EXPERIENCE?

The Son of God, who loved me and gave Himself for me. . .
GALATIANS 2:20

Think what faith in Jesus Christ claims and provides—He can present us faultless before the throne of God, inexpressibly pure, absolutely righteous, and profoundly justified.

We must continually focus and firmly place our faith in Jesus Christ. Our faith must be in the One from whom our salvation springs. We can never *experience* Jesus Christ or selfishly bind Him in the confines of our own hearts. Our faith must be built on strong, determined confidence in Him.

DISCOVERING DIVINE DESIGN

"As for me, being on the way, the LORD led me."

GENESIS 24:27

If we are born of God, we will see His guiding hand and give Him the credit.

We can all see God in exceptional things, but it requires the growth of spiritual discipline to see God in every detail. Never believe that the so-called random events of life are anything less than God's appointed order. Be ready to discover His divine designs anywhere and everywhere.

"WHAT IS THAT TO YOU?"

"But Lord, what about this man?" . . .
"What is that to you?
You follow Me."

JOHN 21:21–22

Y ou put your hand right in front of God's
permissive will to stop it, and then God
says, "What is that to you?" Is there stagnation in
your spiritual life? Get into God's presence and
find out the reason for it. You will possibly find
it is because you have been interfering in the life
of another—advising when you had no right to
advise. When you do have to give advice to another
person, God will advise through you with the direct
understanding of His Spirit.

STILL HUMAN!

Whatever you do, do all to the glory of God.

1 CORINTHIANS 10:31

To do even the most humbling tasks to the glory of God takes the Almighty God incarnate working in us. To be utterly unnoticeable requires God's Spirit in us making us absolutely humanly His. The true test of a saint's life is not successfulness but faithfulness on the human level of life. We tend to set up success in Christian work as our purpose, but our purpose should be to display the glory of God.

THE ETERNAL GOAL

*"By Myself I have sworn, says the LORD,
because you have done this thing. . .blessing I will bless you."*

GENESIS 22:16–17

When Jesus says, "Come," I simply come; when He says, "Let go," I let go; when He says, "Trust God in this matter," I trust. This work of obedience is the evidence that the nature of God is in me.

God will never be real to me until I come face-to-face with Him in Jesus Christ. Then I will know and can boldly proclaim, "In all the world, my God, there is none but Thee, there is none but Thee."

WINNING INTO FREEDOM

*"Therefore if the Son makes you free,
you shall be free indeed."*

JOHN 8:36

Stop listening to the tyranny of your individual natural life and win freedom into the spiritual life.

The *Savior* has set us free from sin, but this is the freedom that comes from being set free from myself *by the Son.* We tend to rely on our own energy instead of being energized by the power that comes from identification with Jesus.

"WHEN HE HAS COME"

"And when He has come,
He will convict the world of sin."

JOHN 16:8

Forgiveness doesn't merely mean that I am saved from hell and have been made ready for heaven (no one would accept forgiveness on that level). Forgiveness means that I am forgiven into a newly created relationship which identifies me with God in Christ. The miracle of redemption is that God turns me, the unholy one, into the standard of Himself, the Holy One. He does this by putting into me a new nature, the nature of Jesus Christ.

THE FORGIVENESS OF GOD

In Him we have. . .the forgiveness of sins.

EPHESIANS 1:7

Forgiveness is the divine miracle of grace. The cost to God was the Cross of Christ. To forgive sin, while remaining a holy God, this price had to be paid. The only way we can be forgiven is by being brought back to God through the atonement of the Cross. God's forgiveness is possible only in the supernatural realm.

Once you realize all that it cost God to forgive you, you will be held as in a vise, constrained by the love of God.

"IT IS FINISHED!"

"I have finished the work which You have given Me to do."
JOHN 17:4

The death of Jesus Christ is the fulfillment in history of the very mind and intent of God. There is no place for seeing Jesus Christ as a martyr. His death was not something that happened *to* Him—something that might have been prevented. His death was the very reason He came.

God forgives sin only because of the death of Christ. God could forgive people in no other way than by the death of His Son, and Jesus is exalted as Savior because of His death.

SHALLOW AND PROFOUND

*Therefore, whether you eat or drink,
or whatever you do, do all to the glory of God.*

1 CORINTHIANS 10:31

Beware of allowing yourself to think that the shallow aspects of life are not ordained by God; they are ordained by Him equally as much as the profound. We sometimes refuse to be shallow, not out of our deep devotion to God but because we wish to impress other people with the fact that we are not shallow. This is a sure sign of spiritual pride. Beware of posing as a profound person—God became a baby.

The Distraction of Contempt

Have mercy on us, O Lord, have mercy on us!
For we are exceedingly filled with contempt.

Psalm 123:3

Our state of mind is powerful in its effects. It can be the enemy that penetrates right into our soul and distracts our mind from God. There are certain attitudes we should never dare to indulge. If we do, we will find they have distracted us from faith in God. Until we get back into a quiet mood before Him, our faith is of no value, and our confidence in the flesh and in human ingenuity is what rules our lives.

DIRECTION OF FOCUS

Behold, as the eyes of servants look to the hand of their masters. . .so our eyes look to the LORD our God.

PSALM 123:2

Just as the eyes of a servant are riveted on his master, our eyes should be directed to and focused on God. This is how knowledge of His countenance is gained and how God reveals Himself to us. Our spiritual strength begins to be drained when we stop lifting our eyes to Him. Our stamina is sapped, not so much through external troubles surrounding us but through problems in our thinking.

THE SECRET OF SPIRITUAL CONSISTENCY

But God forbid that I should boast except in the cross of our Lord Jesus Christ.

GALATIANS 6:14

Most of us are not consistent spiritually because we are more concerned about being consistent externally. In the external expression of things, Paul lived in the basement, while his critics lived on the upper level. And these two levels do not begin to touch each other. But Paul's consistency was down deep in the fundamentals. The great basis of his consistency was the agony of God in the redemption of the world, namely, the Cross of Christ.

THE FOCAL POINT OF SPIRITUAL POWER

Except in the cross of our Lord Jesus Christ. . .

GALATIANS 6:14

Pay attention to the external Source and the internal power will be there. We lose power because we don't focus on the right thing. Concentrate on God's focal point. We have to focus on the great point of spiritual power—the Cross. If we stay in contact with that center of power, its energy is released in our lives.

THE CONSECRATION OF SPIRITUAL POWER

By whom the world has been crucified to me, and I to the world. . .

GALATIANS 6:14

We must never allow anything to interfere with the consecration of our spiritual power. Consecration (being dedicated to God's service) is our part; sanctification (being set apart from sin and being made holy) is God's part. We must make a deliberate determination to be interested only in what God is interested. The way to make that determination is to ask yourself, "Is this the kind of thing in which Jesus Christ is interested?"

THE RICHES OF THE DESTITUTE

Being justified freely by His grace...

ROMANS 3:24

The greatest spiritual blessing we receive is when we come to the knowledge that we are destitute. Until we get there, our Lord is powerless. He can do nothing for us as long as we think we are sufficient in and of ourselves. We must enter into His kingdom through the door of destitution. As long as we are "rich," particularly in the area of pride or independence, God can do nothing for us.

THE SUPREMACY OF JESUS CHRIST

"He will glorify Me."

JOHN 16:14

The New Testament example of the Christian experience is that of a personal, passionate devotion to the Person of Jesus Christ. Every other kind of so-called Christian experience is detached from the Person of Jesus. There is no regeneration—no being born again into the kingdom in which Christ lives and reigns supreme. There is only the idea that He is our pattern. He is salvation itself; He is the gospel of God!

"BY THE GRACE OF GOD I AM WHAT I AM"

His grace toward me was not in vain.

1 CORINTHIANS 15:10

The things that sound humble before God may sound exactly the opposite to people. To say, "Thank God, I know I am saved and sanctified," is in God's eyes the purest expression of humility. It means you have so completely surrendered yourself to God that you know He is true. Never worry about whether what you say sounds humble before others or not. But always be humble before God, and allow Him to be your all in all.

THE LAW AND THE GOSPEL

For whoever shall keep the whole law,
and yet stumble in one point,
he is guilty of all.

JAMES 2:10

The moral law does not consider our weaknesses as human beings. It simply demands that we be absolutely moral. The moral law never changes, either for the highest of society or for the weakest in the world. It is enduring and eternally the same. The moral law, ordained by God, does not make itself weak to the weak by excusing our shortcomings. It remains absolute for all time and eternity.

CHRISTIAN PERFECTION

*Not that I have already attained,
or am already perfected. . .*

PHILIPPIANS 3:12

Christian perfection is not, and never can be, human perfection. Christian perfection is the perfection of a relationship with God that shows itself to be true even amid the seemingly unimportant aspects of human life. God's purpose is not to perfect me to make me a trophy in His showcase; He is getting me to the place where He can use me. Let Him do what He wants.

"NOT BY MIGHT, NOR BY POWER"

*And my speech and my preaching were not
with persuasive words of human wisdom,
but in demonstration of the Spirit and of power.*

1 CORINTHIANS 2:4

Once you are rooted in reality, nothing can shake you. If your faith is in experiences, anything that happens is likely to upset that faith. But nothing can ever change God or the reality of redemption. Base your faith on that, and you are as eternally secure as God Himself. Once you have a personal relationship with Jesus Christ, you will never be moved again.

THE LAW OF OPPOSITION

"To him who overcomes. . ."

REVELATION 2:7

Life without war is impossible in the natural or the supernatural realm. It is a fact that there is a continuing struggle in the physical, mental, moral, and spiritual areas of life.

Anything which is not spiritual leads to my downfall. I must learn to fight against and overcome the things that come against me, and in that way produce the balance of holiness. Then it becomes a delight to meet opposition. Holiness is the balance between my nature and the law of God as expressed in Jesus Christ.

"THE TEMPLE OF THE HOLY SPIRIT"

"Only in regard to the throne will I be greater than you."
GENESIS 41:40

I am accountable to God for the way I control my body under His authority. Every Christian can have his body under absolute control for God.

What I must decide is whether or not I will agree with my Lord and Master that my body will indeed be His temple. Once I agree, all the rules, regulations, and requirements of the law concerning the body are summed up for me in this revealed truth—my body is "the temple of the Holy Spirit."

"MY RAINBOW IN THE CLOUD"

"I set My rainbow in the cloud, and it shall be for the sign
of the covenant between Me and the earth."

GENESIS 9:13

It is the will of God that human beings should get into a right-standing relationship with Him, and His covenants are designed for this purpose.

When I have really transacted business with God on the basis of His covenant, there is no sense of personal achievement—no human ingredient at all. Instead, there is a complete overwhelming sense of being brought into union with God, and my life is transformed.

REPENTANCE

For godly sorrow produces repentance leading to salvation.
2 CORINTHIANS 7:10

The foundation of Christianity is repentance. Strictly speaking, a person cannot repent when he chooses—repentance is a gift of God. The old Puritans used to pray for "the gift of tears." If you ever cease to understand the value of repentance, you allow yourself to remain in sin. Examine yourself to see if you have forgotten how to be truly repentant.

THE IMPARTIAL POWER OF GOD

*For by one offering He has perfected forever
those who are being sanctified.*

HEBREWS 10:14

No matter who or what we are, God restores us to right standing with Himself only by means of the death of Jesus Christ. God does this not because Jesus pleads with Him to do so but because He died. It cannot be earned, just accepted. All the pleading for salvation which deliberately ignores the Cross of Christ is useless. It is knocking at a door other than the one which Jesus has already opened. There is unlimited entrance His way.

THE OPPOSITION OF THE NATURAL

And those who are Christ's have crucified the flesh with its passions and desires.

GALATIANS 5:24

The natural life is not spiritual, and it can be made spiritual only through sacrifice. If we do not purposely sacrifice the natural, the supernatural can never become natural to us. There is no high or easy road. Each of us has the means to accomplish it entirely in his own hands. It is not a question of praying but of sacrificing, and thereby performing His will.

THE OFFERING OF THE NATURAL

*Abraham had two sons: the one by a bondwoman,
the other by a freewoman.*

GALATIANS 4:22

The natural can be turned into the spiritual only through sacrifice. God's perfect will was for the natural to be changed into the spiritual through obedience. Sin is what made it necessary for the natural to be sacrificed.

Some of us are trying to offer up spiritual sacrifices to God before we have sacrificed the natural. The only way we can offer a spiritual sacrifice to God is to "present [our] bodies a living sacrifice" (Romans 12:1).

INDIVIDUALITY

"If anyone desires to come after Me, let him deny himself."
MATTHEW 16:24

Individuality is the hard outer layer surrounding the inner spiritual life. Individuality shoves others aside, separating and isolating people. When we confuse individuality with the spiritual life, we remain isolated. This shell of individuality is God's created natural covering designed to protect the spiritual life. But our individuality must be yielded to God so that our spiritual life may be brought forth into fellowship with Him.

PERSONALITY

"That they may be one just as We are one. . ."

JOHN 17:22

Personality is the unique, limitless part of our life that makes us distinct from everyone else. It is too vast for us even to comprehend. An island in the sea may be just the top of a large mountain, and our personality is like that island. We don't know the great depths of our being; therefore, we cannot measure ourselves. We start out thinking we can but soon realize that there is really only one Being who fully understands us, and that is our Creator.

INTERCESSORY PRAYER

Men always ought to pray and not lose heart.

LUKE 18:1

True intercession involves bringing the person, or the circumstance that seems to be crashing in on you, before God until you are changed by His attitude toward that person or circumstance. People describe intercession by saying, "It is putting yourself in someone else's place." That is not true! Intercession is putting yourself in God's place; it is having His mind and His perspective.

THE GREAT LIFE

"Peace I leave with you, My peace I give to you. . . .
Let not your heart be troubled."

JOHN 14:27

Our attitude must be one of complete reliance on God. Once we get to that point, there is nothing easier than living the life of a saint. We encounter difficulties when we try to usurp the authority of the Holy Spirit.

Any problem that comes while I obey God increases my delight, because I know that my Father knows and cares, and I can watch and anticipate how He will unravel my problems.

"APPROVED TO GOD"

Be diligent to present yourself approved to God,
a worker who does not need to be ashamed,
rightly dividing the word of truth.

2 TIMOTHY 2:15

If you cannot express yourself well on each of your beliefs, work and study until you can. Try to state to yourself what you believe to be the absolute truth of God, and you will be allowing God the opportunity to pass it on through you to someone else.

Always make it a practice to stir your own mind thoroughly to think through what you have easily believed.

WRESTLING BEFORE GOD

Therefore take up the whole armor of God. . .praying always.
EPHESIANS 6:13, 18

You must learn to wrestle *against* the things that hinder your communication with God, and wrestle in prayer *for* other people. Wrestling before God makes an impact in His kingdom. If you ask me to pray for you, and I am not complete in Christ, my prayer accomplishes nothing. But if I am complete in Christ, my prayer brings victory all the time. Prayer is effective only when there is completeness.

REDEMPTION—CREATING THE NEED IT SATISFIES

*But the natural man does not receive
the things of the Spirit of God,
for they are foolishness to him.*

1 CORINTHIANS 2:14

God cannot give until a man asks. It is not that He wants to withhold something from us, but that is the plan He has established for the way of redemption. As redemption creates the life of God in us, it also creates the things which belong to that life. The only thing that can possibly satisfy the need is what created the need. This is the meaning of redemption—it creates and it satisfies.

TEST OF FAITHFULNESS

*And we know that all things work together
for good to those who love God.*

ROMANS 8:28

God may cause our circumstances to suddenly fall apart, which may bring the realization of our unfaithfulness to Him for not recognizing that He had ordained the situation. This is where the test of our faithfulness comes. If we will just learn to worship God even during the difficult circumstances, He will change them for the better very quickly if He so chooses.

THE FOCUS OF OUR MESSAGE

"I did not come to bring peace but a sword."

MATTHEW 10:34

I f you are sensitive to God's way, your message as His servant will be merciless and insistent, cutting to the very root. Otherwise, there will be no healing. We must drive the message home so forcefully that a person cannot possibly hide but must apply its truth. Deal with people where they are until they begin to realize their true need. Then hold high the standard of Jesus for their lives.

THE RIGHT KIND OF HELP

"I, if I am lifted up from the earth,
will draw all peoples to Myself."

JOHN 12:32

Our only priority must be to present Jesus Christ crucified—to lift Him up all the time. If the worker himself believes in Jesus Christ and is trusting in the reality of redemption, his words will be compelling to others. What is extremely important is for the worker's simple relationship with Jesus Christ to be strong and growing. His usefulness to God depends on that, and that alone.

EXPERIENCE OR GOD'S REVEALED TRUTH?

We have received. . .the Spirit who is from God,
that we might know the things that have been
freely given to us by God.

1 CORINTHIANS 2:12

My experiences are not worth anything unless they keep me at the Source of truth—Jesus Christ.

Be relentless and hard on yourself if you are in the habit of talking about the experiences you have had. Faith based on experience is not faith; faith based on God's revealed truth is the only faith there is.

THE DRAWING OF THE FATHER

*"No one can come to Me unless the Father
who sent Me draws him."*

JOHN 6:44

Everyone has been created with the ability
to reach out beyond his own grasp. But it is
God who draws me, and my relationship to Him
in the first place is an inner, personal one, not
an intellectual one. I come into the relationship
through the miracle of God and through my own
will to believe. Then I begin to get an intelligent
appreciation and understanding of the wonder of
the transformation in my life.

SHARING IN THE ATONEMENT

*But God forbid that I should boast except
in the cross of our Lord Jesus Christ.*

GALATIANS 6:14

The great privilege of discipleship is that I can commit myself under the banner of His Cross, and that means death to sin. You must get alone with Jesus and either decide to tell Him that you do not want sin to die out in you, or that at any cost you want to be identified with His death. When you act in confident faith in what our Lord did on the Cross, a supernatural identification with His death takes place immediately.

THE HIDDEN LIFE

Your life is hidden with Christ in God.

COLOSSIANS 3:3

The Spirit of God testifies to and confirms the simple, but almighty, security of the life that "is hidden with Christ in God." We talk as if living a sanctified life were the most uncertain and insecure thing we could do. Yet it is the most secure thing possible, because it has Almighty God in and behind it. The most dangerous and unsure thing is to try to live without God.

HIS BIRTH AND OUR NEW BIRTH

Behold, the virgin shall conceive and bear a Son,
and shall call His name Immanuel.

ISAIAH 7:14

Jesus Christ was born *into* this world, not *from* it. He did not emerge out of history; He came into history from the outside. His life is the highest and the holiest entering through the most humble of doors.

Just as our Lord came into human history from outside it, He must also come into me from outside. The evidence of the new birth is that I yield myself so completely to God that "Christ is formed" in me.

"WALK IN THE LIGHT"

If we walk in the light as He is in the light. . .
the blood of Jesus Christ His Son cleanses us from all sin.

1 JOHN 1:7

I must "walk in the light as He is in the light"—
not in the light of my own conscience, but
in God's light. If I will walk there, with nothing
held back or hidden, then this amazing truth
[of 1 John 1:7] is revealed to me. . . . To "walk in the
light" means that everything that is of the darkness
actually drives me closer to the center of the light.

WHERE THE BATTLE IS WON OR LOST

"If you will return, O Israel," says the LORD. . .

JEREMIAH 4:1

Our battles are won or lost in the secret places of our will in God's presence, never in full view of the world. The Spirit of God seizes me and I am compelled to get alone with God and fight the battle before Him. The battle may take one minute or one year, but that will depend on me, not God. However long it takes, I must wrestle with it alone before God. Nothing has any power over someone who has fought the battle before God and won there.

CONTINUOUS CONVERSION

"Unless you are converted and become as little children. . ."
MATTHEW 18:3

We should continue to turn to God as children, being continuously converted every day of our lives. If we trust in our own abilities instead of God's, we produce consequences for which God will hold us responsible. When God through His sovereignty brings us into new situations, we should immediately make sure that our natural life submits to the spiritual, obeying the orders of the Spirit of God.

DESERTER OR DISCIPLE?

*From that time many of His disciples went back
and walked with Him no more.*

JOHN 6:66

O ur tendency is to bask in the memory of the wonderful experience we had when God revealed His will to us. You can never be the same after the unveiling of a truth. That moment marks you either as one who continues on with even more devotion as a disciple of Jesus Christ, or as one who turns to go back as a deserter.

"AND EVERY VIRTUE WE POSSESS"

"All my springs are in you."

PSALM 87:7

God does not take our natural virtues and transform them, because our natural virtues could never even come close to what Jesus Christ wants. No natural love, no natural patience, no natural purity can ever come up to His demands. But as we bring every part of our natural bodily life into harmony with the new life God has placed within us, He will exhibit in us the virtues that were characteristic of the Lord Jesus.

YESTERDAY

The God of Israel will be your rear guard.

ISAIAH 52:12

At the end of the year we turn with eagerness to all that God has for the future, and yet anxiety is apt to arise when we remember our yesterdays. But God is the God of our yesterdays, and He allows the memory of them to turn the past into a ministry of spiritual growth for our future. God reminds us of the past to protect us from a very shallow security in the present.

INDEX

18:3—12/28

20:22—9/12

20:28—2/23

26:36, 38—4/5

26:40—9/5

26:46—2/18

28:18-19—10/14

28:19—10/27

Mark

1:17—6/13

4:10—1/13

4:34—1/12

6:45—7/28

9:2—10/1

9:9—4/7

9:22—10/2

9:29—10/3

10:21—9/28

10:28—3/12

10:32—3/15

14:6—2/21

16:12—4/9

Luke

1:35—8/8

2:49—8/7

9:57—9/27

9:61—5/30

10:20—4/24, 8/30

11:1—8/28

11:9—6/10

11:10—6/9

12:40—3/29

14:26—7/2

14:28—5/7

18:1—12/13

18:22—8/17

18:23—8/18

18:31—8/3, 8/4, 9/23

18:31, 34—8/5

18:41—2/29

2 Peter

1:4—5/16

1:5—5/10, 6/15

1:5, 7—5/11

1:8—5/12

2:7—12/4

3:10—5/8

4:1—3/27

1 John

1:7—12/26

2:2—10/15

3:2—4/29

5:16—3/31

3 John

7—10/18

Jude

20—10/21

Revelation

1:7—7/29

1:17—5/24

If you enjoyed One-Minute Meditations,
look for these complete editions of
My Utmost for His Highest

Deluxe Christian Classics, 5" x 8"
leather-like hardback, 288 pages, $9.97
ISBN 978-1-57748-914-6

Vest Pocket Edition, 3 ¼" x 6 ⅝" flexible
leather-like, 384 pages, $14.97
ISBN 978-1-59789-935-2

Updated Edition, 4 ¼" x 7" hardback,
400 pages, $14.99
ISBN 978-0-92923-957-6

Updated Edition,
Large Print, 6" x 9" paperback,
400 pages, $14.99
ISBN 978-1-57293-037-7

Available wherever Christian books are sold.